PRAISE FOR MARTIN YAN AND "YAN CAN CO

"Yan has been delighting audiences across the country since 1982 with his patented blend of manic enthusiasm, wacko humor and authentic—and easily recreated—Chinese recipes. Martin Yan is a real gastronomic scholar. His responses make gastronomy human and vibrant....He views food as conversational ecstasy."
San Francisco Chronicle

"Martin Yan really can cook. His show's emphasis is on proper technique, the joys of Pacific Rim cuisine and garden-fresh ingredients."
St. Petersburg Times

"This diminutive Chinese dynamo goes full-tilt both in and out of the kitchen....He's a tremendous chef and kitchen technician. In his hands, a Chinese chef's knife is magical in its speed and grace. And his dishes are surprisingly easy to make."
American Way

"Anyone who has witnessed Yan's razor wit knows it is eclipsed only by his dexterity with a well-honed cleaver as it slices paper-thin rounds of vegetables."
Oakland World-Herald

"His persona is the essence of a good teacher, who is also a 'good performer and a good communicator'."
San Francisco Examiner

"If Yan Can Cook, so can I. Perhaps it's his 'noodling around'...that puts the viewer at ease. Maybe it's the smile, as bright as the lights on the set. Maybe it's the fact that the dishes he whips up go together in just minutes. Everybody seems to have so much fun on the *Yan Can Cook* show on PBS, that it's easy to overlook the fact that Martin Yan is a serious, trained chef, who considers himself first, a cooking teacher, and last—if at all—a celebrity."
Manchester Union Leader

My trusty cleaver has earned me a reputation as a master chopper. But in China, there are master choppers of another kind: the craftsmen who design and carve the stone seals called "chops." Chops come in all shapes and sizes, and each is a hand-made work of art that serves as personal signature. They're used to sign official documents, letters and works of art. My chop bears the characters of my surname, *Jun* (Yan), and my first name, *Won Dar*. Together, these characters mean "culture" and "reach." It is my fondest hope that by reaching out to people all over the world through my cookbooks and the *Yan Can Cook* show, I can share my enthusiasm about the wonders and splendors of Chinese culture.

Won   Jun (Yan)

Dar

MARTIN YAN'S
Culinary Journey Through
China

by Martin Yan

Companion to the
Public Television Series
YAN CAN COOK

Geoffrey Nilsen,
Food Photographer

Bernie Schimbke,
Travel Photographer

YAN CAN COOK
is made possible by
generous grants from
Lee Kum Kee
Circulon
Diamond Walnuts
Vitasoy (Azumaya and Nasoya)

KQED
BOOKS
San Francisco

KQED Vice President for
Publishing & New Ventures:
    Mark K. Powelson

Publisher:
    Pamela Byers
Managing Editor:
    Linda Brandt
Writer:
    Stephen Siegelman
Book Designer & Art Director:
    Traci Shiro
Travel Photographer:
    Bernie Schimbke
Food Photographer:
    Geoffrey Nilsen
Food Stylist:
    Erez
Prop Stylist:
    Bernie Schimbke
Photography Chef:
    Carl Abbott
Chinese Culinary Consultant:
    Bernice Chuck Fong
Food Photography Coordinator:
    Tina Salter
Illustrator:
    Richard Shiro
Cover Design:
    Traci Shiro
Cover Photograph:
    Paul Grebliunas/Tony Stone
    Images
Cover Portrait:
    George Selland
Printing Services by Penn&Ink

KQED President & CEO:
    Mary G. F. Bitterman

Text © 1995 by Martin Yan
Photos © 1995 by KQED, Inc.

Educational and non-profit groups wishing to order this book at attractive quantity
discounts may contact: KQED Books & Tapes, 2601 Mariposa St., San Francisco,
CA 94110.

Yan, Martin. 1948-
    Martin Yan's culinary journey through China / Martin Yan : food
photography by Geoffrey Nilsen : travel photography by Bernie
Schimbke
       p. cm.
    Companion to the Public Television series Yan Can Cook.
    Includes index.
    ISBN 0-912333-64-2
    1. Cookery, Chinese. 2. Cookery--China. 3. China--Description
and travel.   I. Yan Can Cook (Television program)   II. Title.
TX724.5.C5Y2834   1995
641.6951--dc20   95-18719
                                                                          CIP

ISBN 0-912333-64-2

Printed in Hong Kong
10 9 8 7 6 5 4 3 2 1

On the cover: "Cormorant fishing at sunset, Guangxi Province,"
© Paul Grebliunas/Tony Stone Images

Distributed to the trade by Publishers Group West

MARTIN YAN ACKNOWLEDGMENT

There's an old Chinese saying, "for a true friend, a thousand cups of wine are not enough." And for all of my wonderful friends and collaborators who helped turn my dream of a culinary journey through China into a reality—this beautiful cookbook and the public television series, *Yan Can Cook: The Best of China*—a thousand thanks arenot enough.

My journey would not have been possible without the support and hard work of my international crew: Director, James Lingwood; Producer, James Fu; Cinematographer, Paul Dallwitz; Editor, Mitch Wood; Ah Lun, Ah Fung, and my personal assistant, Stephanie Jan. We joined together as collaborators and ended up feeling like a family. I will never forget the precious times we shared together.

I also want to thank my dear friends and colleagues at KQED-TV, San Francisco, my television home for the past 12 years. To the production team—Deanne Hamilton and gayle k. yamada, our executive producers; Linda Brandt, our series producer; Tina Salter and Kate Zilavy, our associate producers; Katherine Russell, Director; Linda Giannecchini, Assistant Director, and our outstanding camera and technical crew— a hearty thank you for another job well done. It's your hard work that makes me look good! I'm grateful to my good friends Steve Siegelman, who polishes my scripts and makes me sound great in the location segments, and Ivan Lai, whose writing enriches the intellectual content of the series.

If Yan "Can Cook", I owe a debt of gratitude to the many cooking professionals who work long hours behind the scenes in the studio: Carl Abbott, chef and kitchen manager; Bernie Schimbke, prop and food stylist; my dear friends Rhoda Yee, Gladys Lee, Bernice Chuck Fong, Joseph Strebler, Christine Swett, Helen Soehalim, Mike Pleiss, Vivienne Marsh and Carol Ritchie; and the volunteers who gave generously of their time and skills—Jack Ervin, Christine Wolf and Robin Basdeo. The fact that we managed to tape 39 shows in 15 days is a tribute to your dedication.

We were most fortunate to enlist the help of three of the finest Chinese restaurants in northern California—Wu Kong and Harbor Village of San Francisco, and Chef Chu's of Los Altos—and the very talented and artistic Chef James Leung.

For helping me create this wonderful book, I am indebted to my publishers, Mark Powelson and Pam Byers of KQED Books; and to Linda Brandt, managing editor; Steve Siegelman, writer *extraordinaire*; and Traci Shiro, designer and art director. My thanks to Bernie Schimbke, travel photographer; Geoffrey Nilsen, food photographer; and Erez, food stylist, for the beautiful images that help bring my culinary journey to life. And to Jan Nix, Jennifer Yuen Louie, Helen Soehalim and Virginia Bast for their tireless dedication in testing and perfecting my recipes.

And finally, to my better half, Sue, thank you for your constant support and patience. You're the best.

In China, we say, "The wise man recognizes work as a privilege, not a chore." As I travel all over the world, the warmth and affection of my loyal readers and viewers make my work a wonderful privilege and a source of endless joy. My most heartfelt thanks to you all.

—M.Y.

Table of Contents

Sichuan

The Journey
In Search of Lotus Roots, Culinary Roots

Let's try a little mind-reading game. Close your eyes for a moment and think about eating a great Chinese meal. The appetizing aromas, the intense flavors, the bright colors and contrasting textures. OK, you can open your eyes now.

In the picture you imagined, you were sitting at a round table in your favorite Chinese restaurant, not in the comfort of your own dining room.

and the *Simple Joys of Chinese Cooking.*

Am I right? I knew it! How did I guess? Years of practice. If you're like most of the people I meet as I travel around the world, you're intrigued by Chinese cuisine. But I'll bet you go *out* to eat Chinese food. Maybe you think it's just too much trouble to prepare at home. Or you worry that you'll have to buy some weird root vegetable and you won't know which part to cook and which

My mom wouldn't know a measuring cup if it hit her on the head. She has no recipes or cookbooks. She follows her senses—and her sense of humor.

part to throw away. Perhaps you feel a bit intimidated by all those complicated steps and mysterious techniques—each one an opportunity to incinerate your family's dinner, warp your wok and wind up ordering take-out. Banish those thoughts from your mind. They couldn't be further from the truth.

Now let me tell you what *I* picture when I daydream about the food of China. For starters, I'm about five years old. It's a rainy gray morning in a suburb of the southern Chinese city of Guangzhou (Canton). Today is a special occasion: the start of the Chinese new year. I'm sitting on the floor under the table in my family's tiny kitchen, listening to the rain come down, watching my mother cook. It's the original *Yan Can Cook* show, and to this day, it's still the best cooking show I've ever seen.

The "set" measures about four feet by six feet. No oven, no appliances, nothing fancy. Just the basics. Like any set, this one has only three walls. The fourth wall is the great outdoors. You can walk right out into the garden where you'll find a vegetable patch, fruit trees, ducks, chickens, a pig or two, even a well and a fish pond.

There's a wood-fired burner topped with a built-in cast-iron wok, blackened and shiny as lacquer from years of use. A cutting board made from a cross-section of a log sits on the counter under a shelf loaded with jars of seasonings, preserved vegetables and pickles. A well-worn cleaver and a few basic tools are close at hand.

No, this isn't the 1800s! I'm old, but not that old! Let's just say that the kind of cooking I was brought up on has remained basically unchanged for thousands of years, and leave it at that.

At the center of this tiny command post is a short, wiry woman, shouting out orders, gesturing wildly and running around so fast it makes me dizzy. That's my mom. Perhaps you've noticed the family resemblance.

Look at her go! Somehow, without stopping to catch her breath, she's whipping up an enormous feast for all our family and friends. Everybody's sitting in the other room laughing and talking. Not mom. She's all business as she deftly transforms a slab of pork into a fine purée, chopping two-fisted with a pair of rapid-fire cleavers.

Now she's adding ginger, garlic and mushrooms to make a savory filling, patting it onto slices of blanched lotus root and flinging them into hot oil. I watch quietly from my post under the table as the lotus patties begin to puff, and before long, they're transformed into my favorite comfort food, the crispy, golden fritters called *Kai Xiang Lian Du Pin*. And the whole time, I'm thinking, "I can do that."

As a kid, I had two passions: practicing martial arts and sitting for hours under that table watching my mom at work. It was as if we both knew right from the start that I was going to become a cook. Every so often, she'd yell out instructions at me over the clanging of the cleaver and the wok: "Remember: 'Hot wok, warm oil.' The oil has to be just right. Too cold, and everything gets greasy. Too hot and the outside gets burned. Watch how the bubbles form on the surface. Cooking is like dancing. You have to stay on your toes and move fast!"

Over the years, I've had the honor of working alongside many Chinese master chefs and cooking teachers. But to this day, my mom is still the greatest natural-born cook I have ever known. Her food is more than sustenance. It's what food is at its best in Chinese families, a nourishing symbol of well-being, harmony and

The "set" of the original *Yan Can Cook* show— a tiny kitchen in Guangzhou.

family connection. It's healthy, simple, honest food, that comes right from the earth. And that's what inspired this book.

You see, my mom wouldn't know a measuring cup if it hit her on the head. She has no recipes or cookbooks. She cooks by instinct and follows her senses—including her sense of humor. And with her as my inspiration, I try to remind myself and my students and television audiences all over the world that cooking is so much more than just recipes and rules. It's all about instincts. It's about improvisation and discovery and having fun. And most of all, it's about simplicity.

Sure, I love a great Chinese restaurant meal as much as anyone. And I spent years as a student, a chef's apprentice and a professional chef perfecting that very specialized art form. But the food I still love best

Sharing a meal with family in my old neighborhood in Guangzhou.

is the pure, simple cooking of the Chinese home. And the more I learn about the essential principles of Chinese cuisine, the more I understand that they're always the same, whether you're preparing a 24-course banquet or a midnight bowl of porridge or noodles. What makes any Chinese meal remarkable is a natural balance of flavor, aroma, color, and texture.

I'm not going to pretend to tell you how to create a grand banquet for 100 people, or even how to make a meal that rivals what you'd find in an outstanding Chinese restaurant (although you will find versions of some of your favorite restaurant-style dishes here). There are plenty of wonderful cookbooks that handle that job well. But most of them are written for experienced cooks.

What I try to present in the *Yan Can Cook* show and what I'm going to show you here are dishes you can cook for your family for dinner tonight, with minimal equipment, a few simple ingredients and some very easy techniques. Don't get me wrong: this isn't watered-down Chinese cooking. It's my interpretation of simple, authentic home-style recipes, adapted for western home cooks.

WHAT'S OLD IS WHAT'S NEW

Why should you be interested in these recipes? Because they represent a whole philosophy of eating that has sustained a quarter of the world's population for thousands of years—and because many Americans are discovering that this philosophy is right in line with the way they want to eat today. More fresh vegetables and grains. A healthy balance of proteins and carbohydrates. Less fat. Quick, spontaneous and convenient preparations. Foods that are exciting and intensely flavored. And most importantly, cooking that does more than fill you up—cooking that satisfies the senses and the soul. My mom is delighted. She thinks everybody is finally following her advice!

And in a way, she's right. Ten years ago, whenever I taught a class or came up with a recipe, I was constantly suggesting substitutions for Chinese ingredients because people couldn't find them at the grocery store. But all that is changing, and my job is getting easier every day! A wonderful array of authentic Asian products, from prepared sauces to ingredients like noodles, dried mushrooms, and fresh produce has exploded onto the market during the last decade.

Park your shopping cart in front of the Asian section of your supermarket and open your mind to a new world of adventure and exploration. Buy a few things you've never tried—a bottle of chili garlic sauce, a package of dried bean curd skins, some salted black beans. Take them home and start experimenting. Check the glossary of this book if you need a little encouragement. Before long, you'll be tasting something you won't believe you made yourself.

That's a lot of words to say a simple message. Chinese cooking is easier than you think. And this book comes with my personal guarantee: If Yan can, you can!

Park your shopping cart in front of the Asian section of your supermarket and open your mind to a new world of adventure and exploration.

How to Eat a Country:

Repeat after me: *Chi le fan mei you?* That's one of the most common Chinese greetings. And what do you suppose it means? Hello? How are you? Nice to see you? No. It means "have you eaten yet?"

That greeting says a lot about the role food plays in Chinese culture. Chinese people spend an average of 40% of their income on food. Every region has its own delicacies—from bird's tongues to fresh-water seaweed to snake meat. Whatever they are, people are passionate about them, and they'll go to any length and expense to enjoy them on special occasions.

Food is always a sure-fire conversation starter. The Chinese talk about where and what they're going to eat all day. Then when they're finally eating, they talk about what they'll have for their next meal! Food talk was all I heard growing up. Maybe that's why I decided to make a living talking about food myself!

And sharing opinions about food is just the beginning. The food itself must be shared, too. The importance of sharing is instilled in Chinese children from an early age. It would be unthinkable to order a dish all to yourself in a restaurant in China—or to serve a dish to a single person at home. Everything is intended to be experienced and discussed by all the guests. That's why many Chinese tables are round—so you can see and talk to everyone, and everyone has equal access to the food at the center of the table.

It's all about togetherness. In China, family units stay together with many generations living under one roof. After thousands of years, that's still the way it's done, and I'm convinced that cooking and eating are a huge part of the thread that holds the Chinese social fabric together.

Over the years, I've shared a lot of meals with a lot of people in China. These days, I spend about a third of my time there, meeting, greeting and, of course, eating. Between teaching and consulting, I travel so much, I've thought about setting up a frequent flyer account for me, and a frequent *fryer* account for my wok!

Most of my travel to the

A Culinary Journey

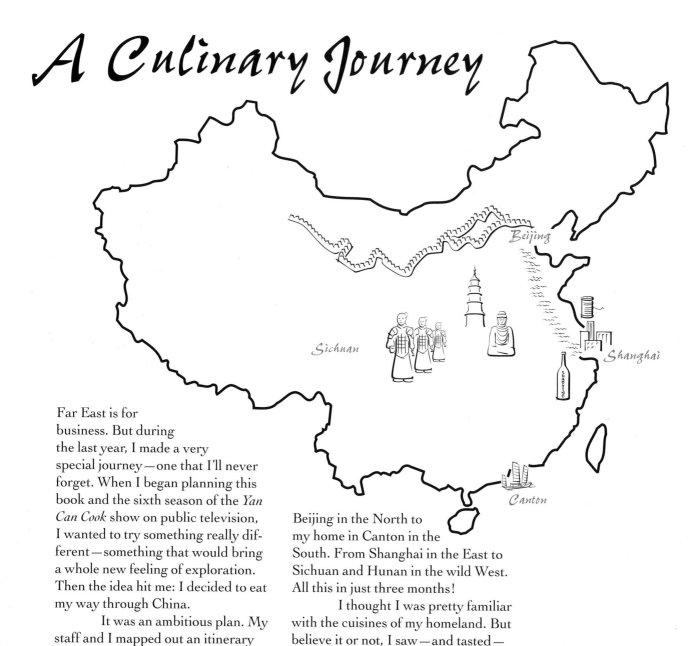

Far East is for business. But during the last year, I made a very special journey—one that I'll never forget. When I began planning this book and the sixth season of the *Yan Can Cook* show on public television, I wanted to try something really different—something that would bring a whole new feeling of exploration. Then the idea hit me: I decided to eat my way through China.

It was an ambitious plan. My staff and I mapped out an itinerary that would take us all the way from Beijing in the North to my home in Canton in the South. From Shanghai in the East to Sichuan and Hunan in the wild West. All this in just three months!

I thought I was pretty familiar with the cuisines of my homeland. But believe it or not, I saw—and tasted— more of China in that short time than I

A 65,000-mile odyssey: biking through Beijing; thumbing a ride on the road to Shanghai; navigating the canals of Souzhou.

have in my entire life. The book you are holding is a record of that trip: the recipes and inspirations I collected, the foods I discovered, and the people and traditions I encountered.

When all was said and done, we logged more than 65,000 miles over land, sea, air and waterways. Just for fun, we gave ourselves the challenge of using every means of transportation we could find: plane, train, bus, car, boat, gondola, bicycle, tricycle, pedi-cab, horse and donkey. I even tried hitch-hiking in the 115°

heat one afternoon, but no one would stop. It seems the Chinese don't recognize the "thumbs up" signal!

Along the way, we met thousands of people, made hundreds of friends, and ate more food than you would believe. For me, it was the trip of a lifetime: a culinary journey that brought me back to my roots in a way I'd never thought possible. It was a powerful experience. Often moving (usually fast-moving!), sometimes hilarious, and always enjoyable and educational.

And believe me, it was no pleasure cruise. I wanted to get a feel for the real lives of people at work, so I decided to work with them. I cooked side-by-side with master chefs in some of the greatest restaurants in China. I prepared a simple meal with the monks in the kitchen of the Shaolin Monastery. I even spent an evening grilling skewers of spicy lamb in a takeout food stall in the open-air market outside Beijing's Forbidden City.

Between the big cities, the countryside amazed us with its simple, timeless beauty. We harvested rice in a vast rice paddy near Wuhan, picked fruit on a farm in a tiny village near Louyang, caught fresh fish in Souzhou, herded ducks in a rainstorm at Beijing's largest duck farm, watched wine being made in Shao Hsing, the rice wine capital of China, and learned how to harvest and dry tea leaves at the famous Dragon Well tea plantation near Hangzhou. There were spectacular day-long banquets, impromptu picnics, tea ceremonies, wine tastings, and hours spent exploring the open-air markets.

And everywhere we went, people opened their doors, their kitchens and their tables to us. Ordinary people with an extraordinary talent for turning a little bit of this and that into a perfectly balanced meal.

We scribbled notes and laughed and talked and tasted. And all the while, I kept thinking about one word: simplicity. After years of studying cooking and food science, it's a humbling experience to be served an unforgettable meal that was cooked entirely over a few lumps of coal.

My great crew on the Great Wall.

17

IT'S ALL IN THE BALANCE

What's the key to this remarkable simplicity? It all comes down to the essential principle of balance. As long ago as the 4th Century BC, the Chinese had identified five essential taste sensations—salty, sweet, sour, bitter and spicy-hot. The proper balance and interplay of these tastes creates a cuisine of infinite variety and sophistication. Color and texture, too, are varied to keep things lively and interesting within each dish and throughout the meal.

Add to this the ancient Chinese principle of two opposing forces in balance—yin and yang. Yin represents the feminine, yielding, darker, more mysterious forces, while yang stands for the masculine, harder, brighter and hotter ones.

In the world of food, yin might be cooler, moister, softer foods, like winter melon, asparagus or crab meat. Yang might take the form of chiles, ginger, fried foods or red meat. Yin and Yang are important in combining colors and textures, too: bright colors balancing pale ones, toothsome textures setting off softer ones.

There's no right or wrong attached to Yin and Yang. What's more important, in life, as in food, is creating a dynamic harmony of complementary ingredients.

Chinese cooks feel that balancing these ingredients not only heightens the eating experience, but also keeps the body in a state of equilibrium and good health. But don't panic. It's not like everybody sits around with a set of scales weighing things, or poring over charts and rule books to see which yin goes best with which yang. It's just that the best Chinese food begins with this instinctive sense of contrasting elements in balance.

I have tried to achieve that balance in the recipes in this book, so you can experience it first-hand. I've also kept the ingredient lists short and the methods simple so you can master them easily, and so the true flavors of the food come through. Now, before you get started, let me give you some basic guidelines on equipment, techniques, and cooking methods. Read them first, and you'll find the rest will come naturally.

Tools & Techniques

EVERYDAY CHINA: EQUIPPING YOUR KITCHEN

I'll never forget my first television appearance. It was a freezing winter day in Alberta, Canada, and when I pulled into the parking lot of the TV studio, I discovered that the lock on my trunk had frozen shut. My trusty wok and cleaver and all my equipment were stuck inside!

"The show must go on," I told myself, and I ran into the studio, where, somehow, using a battered skillet, a plastic spatula and some food from the lunchroom, I managed to fill five minutes of air time. I've blanked out most of the experience, but I remember smiling a lot and moving around very fast to avoid collapsing from nervousness.

Why am I telling you this story? To make a simple point. It doesn't take a huge arsenal of equipment to cook Chinese food. Remember my mom with the three-walled kitchen and the wood stove? When in doubt, improvise!

To prepare the recipes in this book, I recommend supplementing your kitchen with a "starter kit," consisting of three basic Chinese cooking tools: a wok, some kind of steamer and a Chinese chef's knife. These tools have evolved over thousands of years, and, when you treat them well, they perform perfectly. As your repertoire expands, you'll find that using the right equipment makes cooking easier, tastier and more fun. Just keep one important rule in mind: never leave anything in your trunk on a cold day!

Taking a turn at the wok in a farmhouse kitchen near Xian.

THE WOK

Wok of Ages

Necessity is the mother of invention. Case in point: the mother of all Chinese cooking utensils, the wok, whose name, meaning "cooking vessel" points to its elemental importance. Many centuries ago, when the wok was born, the necessities in question were limited fuel and food. Cooking had to be done quickly and efficiently.

Originally, the wok was designed to fit into a well in the top of a wood- or coal-burning stove. With its curved, sloping sides, the wok could cook ingredients in a small area of concentrated heat at its center, the part closest to the heat source. Cutting up the ingredients into uniform chunks, and quickly stir-frying them in batches helped conserve energy and make the cooking process even more efficient.

Nutrients, colors, textures and flavors could be kept at their peak because of the short cooking time. Fats and oils, another precious commodity, could be used sparingly, because once a wok is well seasoned, a light drizzle of oil is all that is needed for non-stick cooking. What could be more contemporary than that?

To this day, wok cooking remains the most frequently used technique in the Chinese kitchen. In rural China, you'll still find heavy, cast-iron woks used in the ancient way, recessed in a well over an open fire.

But in urban home kitchens and restaurants, gas burners and electric heating elements have given rise to a more modern kind of wok, the kind you're probably familiar with. Because it sits on the stove top, the modern wok is lighter in weight for easy handling, and comes in a variety of sizes, materials and types.

Once you discover how versatile a wok can be, it might just become the most used piece of cookware you own. You'll find that stir-frying is just the beginning. A wok is great for steaming, deep-frying, braising, stewing, boiling, poaching and even smoking.

Wok shopping on the road to Shao Hsing.

Shopping for a Wok

Finding the best wok for your needs doesn't have to be difficult. Just remember to consider the three S's: shape, size and substance.

Shape
The Bottom Line

Woks can be grouped into two basic types: round-bottomed and flat-bottomed.

Round-bottomed. Originally designed for wood or charcoal burners, round-bottomed woks work well when used over gas burners. You can set the wok directly over the burner grate, or, for greater stability, you can use a perforated, ring-shaped metal wok stand that sits over the burner and holds the wok in place. If you use a stand with sloping sides, which way is right-side up? That depends on your wok and your stove. Position the stand so that the wok sits as close to the heat as possible, and has the greatest exposure to the whole flame.

Flat-bottomed. Originally designed for use with electric burners, these woks can sit right on top of the heating element without a stand. You'll need to experiment with the heat settings on your range to find the heat that works best for quick cooking without burning. Of course, this type of wok works with gas burners, too.

Size
A Matter of Portions and Proportions

For family cooking like the kind presented in this book, a wok measuring 14 inches in diameter is your best bet, and will hold enough food to serve four to six people. For a small family or when cooking for 1 or 2 people, a 12-inch wok is adequate. You can find larger ones ranging from 16 to 30 inches in diameter, but they tend to be heavy and unwieldy for the everyday cook. Take a good look at the size of your stovetop and plan accordingly.

Substance
From Heavy Metal to Light Wok

Traditional Chinese woks made of cast iron are scarcely sold in the U.S. But a variety of excellent lighter-metal woks are available.

Carbon Steel. The time-honored carbon steel wok is made from a disk of steel that has been shaped on a lathe-like contraption. These inexpen-

WOK, STOCK & BARREL

If you don't already own a wok, or if you're thinking of upgrading, you might consider buying one of the many complete wok kits on the market. Most contain everything you need to get started, including a lid, wok stand, spatula, ladle, strainer and steaming rack. It's a modest investment that will have you up and wokking as soon as you open the box.

HANDLE WITH CARE

Woks generally have either two matching loop-shaped handles or one long one with an optional short one on the opposite side. A long handle makes for easy two-handed stir-frying: you can keep one hand on the spatula and one on the handle, moving the wok around as you work. Advanced cooks love to show off by using the long-handled wok to toss ingredients high in the air. It's fun, but try practicing outside, off-heat, with some dried beans first.

sive "spun" or "rolled" steel woks can be identified by the fine rings in the surface of the metal. They retain heat well, and they're lightweight for easy cooking and storing. Traditional hammered-steel woks are also made from carbon steel, but they're difficult to find in the U.S. Carbon steel woks need to be properly seasoned when new (see "Seasoning the Wok" below), and properly cared for.

Stainless Steel. Stainless steel woks, or those made of aluminum and lined with stainless steel, can also be found at a range of prices. These woks are shiny and attractive, but food often sticks to their cooking surface.

Anodized Aluminum. Woks made of anodized aluminum require no seasoning, and many offer a non-stick, scratch-resistant cooking surface. Substantial and durable, they are excellent conductors of heat. They're also easy to clean and care for.

Non-Stick Coatings. Some woks, including many of the electric variety, are coated with a non-stick surface that's easy to clean. It's worth spending a few extra dollars for a wok with a high-quality surface. Use wooden or plastic utensils for cooking and non-abrasive scrubbers for cleanup.

The Eclectic Electric. A relative newcomer to the world of wok cookery is the electric wok, with its built-in heating element and thermostat control. Electric woks are designed for all-purpose use, and they're handy because they free up your stovetop. They're particularly good for deep-frying, braising and steaming, since they heat evenly and allow you to set and maintain exact cooking temperatures. And they're ideal for table-top cooking or for keeping buffet food warm.

Seasoning the Wok

Before using a carbon steel wok, you'll need to remove the protective coating on its surface, and reseal the surface with oil. This process, called *seasoning*, isn't hard to do, and it has its rewards. First, it begins the process of creating a slick, non-stick cooking surface that gets better and better with age and repeated use. Second, it seals out moisture so the metal won't rust.

1. Remove the film of rust-preventive oil that coats most new woks by scrubbing the inside and outside surfaces with warm water, detergent and steel wool or a scouring pad.

2. Rinse the wok thoroughly and set it over medium heat for several minutes to dry.

3. Moisten a paper towel with a little cooking oil. With the wok set over medium heat and holding the towel in an oven mitt, spread the oil evenly over the inside surface of the wok. Add ½ teaspoon of fine salt and continue to rub the entire inside surface. Soon, the wok will begin to darken and smoke. This would be a good time to turn on the exhaust fan.

4. Using fresh changes of paper towels and a bit more oil and salt if the surface begins to look dry, continue wiping the surface of the wok, rubbing firmly to get the oil into the pores of the metal, until the towel comes away reasonably clean. The process can take up to twenty minutes, and varies from wok to wok, so consult the manufacturer's directions.

5. Finally, allow the wok to cool, then wash it in warm water with a soft, nylon brush or pad, and dry it on the stove over heat.

Now you've created the first layer of the seasoned surface. There will be a dark brown area spread over the center of the wok. As you continue to cook with the wok, that brown area will grow, and eventually, the whole wok will become shiny and dark.

Cleaning the Wok

After each use, clean the still-hot wok right away with hot water and little or no soap. To remove persistent burned food, try rubbing the surface of the wok with salt, which acts as a natural abrasive. After cleaning and rinsing, always dry your wok over heat. Towel drying or air drying won't remove all the water from the pores of the metal, and rust can form.

HEY! WHAT'S THAT AMAZING FLAVOR?

There's a mysterious, appetizing flavor that many foods take on when they're cooked in a seasoned wok over high heat—a savory, "wok-charred" taste the Chinese call *wok hey.* That's the mark of a well-seasoned wok—and a seasoned wok chef!

AVOIDING "ACID WOK"

Sauces made with acidic ingredients, like vinegar or tomato, can eat away at the seasoning you've been diligently building up, and your sauce may take on a tinny flavor. For very acidic sauces, you're better off cooking the sauce in a separate, nonreactive saucepan, then quickly tossing it with the ingredients in the wok at the last minute.

Wok-cessories

Whether included with your wok or purchased separately, a few traditional Chinese accessories can make wok cooking more efficient and enjoyable.

Spatula. With its shovel-shaped blade that hugs the curves of the wok, the wok spatula is perfect for stir-frying and scooping food out of the wok. The long handle keeps you from stir-frying your fingertips. It's fun to toss food around with a clanging Chinese spatula, but if you don't have one, an ordinary wooden or plastic one will do the trick.

Skimmer. This is the Chinese version of the western slotted spoon but bigger, normally 6 to 8 inches across. It's most often used for fishing food out of hot oil or water. The kind most commonly sold in the U.S. is a flat wooden or bamboo slat with a wire mesh basket at one end.

Ladle. This one, you know. Chinese ladles are typically a little shallower and wider than western ones because they're designed to match the curve of the wok. You can use a Chinese ladle as a companion to the spatula for stir-frying, or for scooping liquids and cooked foods into and out of the wok.

Chopsticks. Special extra-long wooden chopsticks are another helpful tool for wok cooking. Use them for frying foods, to separate boiling noodles and to snatch bits of food from the wok for tasting.

Lid. The high, dome-shaped or sloped-sided wok lid lets you turn the wok into a steamer, braising pot or smoker. If your wok didn't come with a lid, look for one that's slightly smaller in diameter than the wok, so it sits solidly, just below the wok's rim.

Stir-Fry, Step by Step

You've chosen your wok, seasoned it (if necessary) and set it up in your kitchen. It's time to start putting it to work. Let's start with the #1 wok cooking technique: stir-fry. Here are my secrets for stir-fry success. Of course, every dish is different, and the recipes in this book will give you exact directions. But these are the basic principles that usually apply.

1. *Cutting.* Chop, slice, dice or shred each ingredient in uniform pieces to ensure even cooking.

2. *Seat the Guests.* No kidding! You don't want your piping hot creation to sit at the table getting cold and soggy while you herd your friends and family to the table. (Once you get the hang of the technique, you can make two stir-fries at a time. Meanwhile, it's always wise to plan a menu with other kinds of dishes, like soups and steamed or roasted foods so there's less waiting, and you can sit down to enjoy your own cooking.)

3. *Setup.* Stir-frying is like downhill skiing—once you start, there's no stopping. Read the recipe first, and make sure you have everything cut up, marinated, measured and close at hand. Don't forget the serving plate and the garnish.

4. *Heat First, Oil Second.* Place the empty wok over high heat for a minute or two. When you can feel the heat by lowering your hand slightly into the wok, you're ready to add the oil. Drizzle the oil (it doesn't usually take more than a couple of tablespoons) around the sides of the wok, swirling it to coat the surface. Wait about 15 seconds until the oil is hot before adding other ingredients.

5. *Know Your Orders.* Stir-frying is usually done in batches, and the sequence in which ingredients are added is important. Seasonings like ginger, garlic or chiles are usually added first. Stir-fry for a few seconds before adding the meat. Sometimes the meat is removed before vegetables are added; heartier, denser vegetables usually go in before softer or leafier ones. Let the recipe be your guide.

6. *Stir, Don't Stare.* Use your spatula to flip and toss the food vigorously, breaking up any clumps, so everything cooks evenly without sticking to the wok. I like to give the wok a good shake from time to time to keep everything moving.

7. *Avoid Over-Crowding.* If you use too big a batch of any ingredient, it becomes hard to stir-fry evenly, and the excess moisture may prevent uniform browning. You end up "steam-frying" or "boil-frying."

8. *Sauce.* Many recipes call for a final addition of liquid (such as wine or broth) and/or a prepared sauce (such as soy sauce or oyster sauce). This liquid is sometimes thickened with a mixture of cornstarch and water, depending on the type of sauce desired. Combine the sauce ingredients ahead, and mix the cornstarch with the water. Keep both within easy reach.

9. *Taste.* Don't forget to taste the dish before you put it on the serving plate. Then quickly adjust the seasonings, if necessary, and serve.

10. *Garnish.* This is a little touch that makes a big difference. I like to use a bit of an ingredient that's already in the dish (like an slice of lemon with Lemon Chicken). Keep it simple. Even a sprig of cilantro or a sprinkling of toasted sesame seeds adds a special finish to a dish.

Deep-Frying

Your wok makes a wonderful deep-fryer that heats evenly, uses less oil and is easy to use. Deep-frying has gotten a bad rap in recent years, and it does require a fair amount of oil, but foods that have been properly deep-fried at the right temperature absorb less oil and can be light and crispy, without being greasy.

When foods are added to oil that has been heated to between 330°F and 375°F (check your recipe for exact temperature), the surface of the food is quickly sealed, forming a coating the oil cannot permeate. If the oil is not hot enough, too much oil soaks in. If it's too hot, the outside of the food can burn before the inside is cooked.

Deep-Frying Tips

- Use a flat-bottomed wok (for electric ranges), a round-bottomed wok set securely in a wok stand (for gas ranges) or an electric wok. Make sure the wok is solidly positioned to avoid tipping.

- Pour oil into the wok to a depth of 1½ to 2-inches.

- Heat the oil to the temperature called for in the recipe, checking it with a deep-frying or candy thermometer. If you don't have a thermometer, you can test the temperature by carefully dropping a cube of bread into the oil. The bread should start to sizzle immediately; it will soon be coated with bubbles and begin to turn golden-brown. Or try my chopstick trick: place the tip of a dry wooden chopstick into the bottom of the oil; when tiny bubbles emerge from the end of the chopstick, your oil is ready.

- Be extra careful when placing foods into hot oil to avoid splashing and spattering. Remember—*slide, not slam-dunk!*

- Bring the ingredients you're going to deep-fry to room temperature before adding them to the oil. This will minimize the lowering of the oil temperature and help prevent spattering.

- Add the ingredients in small batches so that the oil doesn't overflow. This also helps maintain a constant oil temperature and promotes even browning.

- Use your wire strainer or a slotted spoon to turn and separate the food as it cooks and to lift it out and transfer it to paper towels for draining.

- Oil used for deep-frying can be reused, although after two to three uses, it will begin to break down. To reuse deep-frying oil, allow it to cool, pour it through a fine mesh strainer to remove particles of food, then store it in an airtight jar in the refrigerator. If, after repeated use, the oil begins to darken, discard it.

Wok-Smoking

In Chinese cooking, smoking is really more a flavoring method than a cooking process. Foods are often marinated before smoking, then placed on a rack in the wok over aromatic ingredients like brown sugar, tea, uncooked rice, star anise or wood chips. Heat is applied to create smoke, which is sealed in by the lid of the smoker.

Typically, food is first cooked by another method, such as pan-frying, steaming or roasting, then smoked to add flavor. You can use any deep, heavy pot with a tight-fitting lid for stovetop smoking, but a wok with a high-domed lid works perfectly. Don't use your best wok, though, since smoking is an intense dry-heat process that can harm a wok's seasoning. An old, battered one will work fine. Give wok-smoking a try. The robust aroma and flavor it gives food can be unforgettable.

Wok-Smoking Tips

- Open some windows, and turn on the exhaust fan.

- Line the wok and the lid with a few layers of aluminum foil, leaving extra foil hanging over the edges.

- Place the aromatic ingredients (tea, brown sugar, etc.) in the bottom of an old wok, and set a rack over them. Choose a rack that will sit stably in the wok, a few inches over the smoking ingredients. You can use a tic-tac-toe shaped smoking/steaming rack (one may have been included with your wok), four heavy chopsticks, arranged in tic-tac-toe fashion, or a wire rack. I've known people who have used everything from a round cake rack to a clean charcoal rack from a round barbecue.

- Heat the wok over high heat until smoke begins to form. Place the food to be smoked on the rack, and immediately cover the wok with the lid. Crimp and fold the foil that's sticking out all around the wok and the lid to seal in the smoke.

THE STEAMER

After stir-frying, steaming is probably the second most common cooking method in China. Traditional Chinese home kitchens don't have ovens, and the steamer helps fill the void. It's used to cook seafood, meats, poultry and vegetables, to make silky steamed custards and to "bake" buns, dumplings and even cakes over moist heat.

Steaming is simply cooking food on a rack above boiling water in a closed cooking vessel. Your trusty wok makes a fine base. To it, you'll need to add some kind of steaming rack, depending on your recipe, and a lid. The rack can be as simple as four chopsticks, placed tic-tac-toe-style a few inches above the boiling water, topped with a plate on which the food is set. You can also use a conventional metal vegetable-steaming rack.

My favorite tool for steaming, though, is the one I grew up with: the old-fashioned but ingenious wok steamer. It's a round, flat basket, made of bamboo, that sits right in the wok, an inch or so above the water.

These steamers have space between the slats on the bottom to let the steam in, and a lid to keep it there. They can be stacked so you can cook several dishes at once. For a 14-inch wok, look for steamer baskets about 12 to 13 inches in diameter.

Bamboo steamers have latticed lids of woven bamboo which let just the right amount of steam escape so condensed water doesn't drip down onto the food. They're so attractive and unusual looking that you can serve food right out of them. Some people prefer a tiered aluminum steamer set, which has a flat, round pan at its base that's designed to hold water. Fans of the aluminum steamer will tell you

In this shop in Sichuan bamboo steamers are still made by hand, the old-fashioned way.

FULL STEAM AHEAD

I'm happy to see that steaming is coming into fashion in the West, because it's one of my favorite cooking methods. The flavors of steamed foods are outstandingly clean, delicate and soothing, their texture moist and tender. Little or no oil is needed for steaming, and most of the vitamins, minerals and natural juices of foods are retained. Steaming is also convenient; you can place food in a steamer and then move on to other things without needing to keep a constant watch over it.

that it's more durable than bamboo, and won't mildew or absorb cooking odors as bamboo can if it's not carefully cleaned and dried.

Whichever steamer you choose, you'll seldom place food directly on the steamer itself. Foods that cook in their own juices—like a whole fish—sit on a heat-resistant plate inside the steamer. Choose one that's slightly smaller than the steamer basket so the steam can rise around it. For dumplings and buns, line the steamer with a damp cloth to prevent sticking. For some preparations, the Chinese line steamer baskets with greens, such as napa cabbage or lettuce leaves.

Steamer Tips

- Check the water level in the bottom of the steamer occasionally. If it's low, add boiling water to avoid lowering the temperature.

- A heat-resistant glass pie plate makes an ideal liner for steaming fish, custards and other foods.

- To steam larger items, like whole fowl, set two cans, emptied, cleaned and with both ends removed, in the bottom of a large Dutch oven with a lid. Add water to half way up the cans, and then use them as a support for a plate or dish on which to place the food.

- Don't get steamed! To avoid burns, always open the steamer with care. Wear oven mitts, and lift the lid so that it points away from you.

THIS IS YOUR KNIFE

Cutting food up in uniform pieces is one of the most important skills to master in Chinese cooking. And once you learn to use an all-purpose Chinese chef's knife, it's easier than you think. If Yan can cut, so can you!

I like to tell my students that the Chinese chef's knife is the original Chinese food processor. It can slice, mince, chop, crush, tenderize and scoop up food—and you can even use the end of the handle to grind spices. Complement it with a smaller paring knife for finer cutting and making garnishes, and you'll be ready for just about anything.

Shop Till You Chop:
Buying a Chinese Chef's Knife

Although the light-weight, all-purpose Chinese chef's knife is sometimes called a cleaver and looks like a western meat cleaver, it's a different tool altogether (and thus should never be used for hacking bones—for that you'll need a heavier one). A good Chinese chef's knife is well-balanced, well-constructed and has a fine sharp blade that holds an edge.

Carbon steel Chinese chef's knives are widely available and easy to sharpen, but they can rust and will discolor acidic foods like onions and lemons. Ordinary stainless steel, on the other hand, can dull quickly. That's why I prefer a high-carbon stainless steel blade, like the signature Martin Yan knife that I designed and use on the *Yan Can Cook* show. High-carbon stainless steel won't discolor food and keeps a fine, sharp edge.

In some high-quality chef's knives, the end of the blade, called the tang (no relation to the Chinese dynasty of the same name!), extends all the way to the end of the handle and is held in place by three rivets. You can also find traditional knives with cylindrical wooden handles. Test the balance of the knife and the comfort of the handle as you hold it. It should feel substantial, yet not so heavy that your hand and wrist will tire quickly.

31

Getting a Grip

Hold the Chinese chef's knife in your writing hand (the Chinese call this the "chopstick hand"). Move your hand all the way up the handle so that your thumb is on one side of the blade and your index finger on the other side. Curling your index finger slightly, grasp the blade firmly between your thumb and index finger. This may feel a bit strange at first, but once you get used to it, you'll find that grasping the blade in this way gives you much more control than simply wrapping all your fingers around the handle.

Use your free hand to hold the food in place, curling your fingertips under. Rest the flat side of the blade alongside the first knuckles of your free hand, and as you slice or chop, slide your free hand along to guide the blade and keep it vertical. To avoid cutting yourself, never uncurl the fingers of your free hand, and never raise the blade higher than the first knuckle. Like I always say, "the idea is to move your fingers, not remove them!" Try not to wiggle the blade while cutting. Use a firm downward and slightly forward motion.

Short Cuts:
Knife Techniques Made Simple

Slicing: Holding the food and Chinese chef's knife firmly, cut straight down, using the knuckles of your free hand as a guide.

Julienne and Shredding: Stack a few slices, and use the slicing technique, cutting straight down through the stack to create sticks. For matchstick julienne, start with ¼-inch slices, and cut them into ¼-inch sticks. To shred food into fine slivers, begin by cutting paper thin slices, then cut across them in the same way to create thin strips.

Dicing: Line sticks up perpendicular to the blade, and slice straight down across them, creating cubes.

Mincing: Start by cutting the ingredient into thin strips, then dice the strips. Hold the knife handle in one hand and, with the other, hold down the tip of the blunt edge of the blade. Using the tip as a pivot, raise and lower the blade in a chopping motion, moving it from side to side to mince everything evenly. Scoop up minced ingredients occasionally, flip them over and keep chopping to ensure even mincing.

Roll Cutting: This technique is used for long vegetables, like carrots or zucchini. It makes attractive chunks and exposes more of the surface area of the vegetable. Hold the blade perpendicular to the board and cut straight down on the diagonal. Then roll the vegetable a quarter turn and cut straight down again at the same diagonal angle. Continue rolling and cutting in this way all along the length of the vegetable.

Parallel Cutting: Used to cut broad, thin slices of meat or vegetables. Lay the food close to the edge of the board with the fingers of your flat free hand on top of it. Angle the Chinese chef's knife so that it's almost parallel to the board, slanting slightly downward. Move it slowly and carefully back and forth to slice the food, paying close attention to avoid cutting your fingers.

Crushing: To crush ginger or garlic, place it near the edge of the cutting board, lay the knife blade flat over it with the blade facing away, and, with

the heel of your free hand, give the side of the blade a good whack.

Tenderizing: Use the blunt edge of the Chinese chef's knife to tenderize meat by pounding it in a criss-cross pattern. It's even more fun to get out your aggressions by turning the blade on its side and slapping the surface of the meat.

Grinding Spices: Most Chinese kitchens are equipped with a mortar and pestle—a stone bowl and club used for crushing and grinding spices. If you don't have one, you can put spices in a small bowl and use the end of the handle of your chef's knife to pound and crush them. A mini-food processor or coffee grinder will also do the trick. Serious spice lovers may want to invest in a second coffee grinder for spice grinding only. They work wonderfully for this purpose, but make sure to label your grinders so you can tell which is which. I once wound up with Sichuan-peppercorn-flavored cappuccino!

HERE'S A SHARP IDEA!
An easy way to slice meat thinly is to partially freeze it (or, if it's frozen, partially thaw it) until it's soft enough to cut, but still firm. You'll find it's a simple matter to slice it into thin strips.

33

Staying on the Cutting Edge:
Care and Cleaning

Wash your chef's knife after each use in warm, soapy water and dry it well. Never put a good knife in the dishwasher. To maintain a sharp edge, I recommend using a traditional knife-sharpening steel.

3. Push the blade downward along the steel, pulling it toward you as you go, until you reach the steel's tip.

1. Hold the steel firmly, placing its tip on a cutting board.

4. Move the blade back up and place its other side against the steel; repeat the sharpening action, moving the blade from the steel's handle to its tip.

5. Repeat two or three times on each side of the blade.

2. Position the knife at a 20° angle to the steel with the blade facing down and the handle of the knife just below the handle of the steel.

If the blade loses its edge and becomes too dull to sharpen with a steel, use a whetstone or have your knife professionaly sharpened by your butcher or at your local cutlery store.

CLAY POT COOKING

With a wok, a steamer and a Chinese chef's knife, you're ready for just about anything. But a traditional Chinese clay pot is one piece of equipment you may want to add to your arsenal just for fun.

Clay pots, also called "sand pots," because they're made from a mixture of sand and clay, have heavy lids and are often encased in a wire mesh to protect them. They're both functional for cooking and beautiful enough for serving soups and stews right at the table. Clay pots are usually glazed on the inside and unglazed on the outside for better heat absorption, making them ideal for braising, simmering, stewing and slow-cooking.

You can find inexpensive clay pots in a variety of shapes and sizes in Chinese specialty shops. But what if you can't find a Chinese specialty shop? You can still achieve great results using any lidded flame-resistant casserole dish.

Clay Pot Tips

Clay pots are fired at a high temperature so they can withstand intense heat. You can place them directly on a gas burner or in the oven; if you're using an electric burner, place a diffuser under the pot. Clay pots are fragile, so follow these guidelines to avoid breakage:

- Never place an empty clay pot directly over heat. Always add some liquid first.

- Allow the pot to cool completely before immersing it in water or placing it on a damp or cold surface.

MORE TECHNIQUES AND TIPS

Here are a few more techniques and basic prep methods that will help you prepare the recipes in this book.

Parboiling

Also known as "blanching" or "water-blanching," parboiling refers to immersing food in boiling water for a few seconds or a few minutes to partially pre-cook it. Once it is removed from the water (use your Chinese strainer or a slotted spoon), the food is usually placed under cold water to stop the cooking process.

Roasting

In China, roasting happens mostly in restaurants, because home kitchens usually don't have ovens. In restaurants, meat is often roasted in large ovens where it can be hung on hooks, allowing air to circulate all around it. You can replicate this effect by roasting on a rack over a foil-lined pan.

Braising

Braising is an ideal way to prepare large cuts of meat that need to cook slowly. The food is first browned over high heat, then slowly stewed in liquid in a heavy, covered pot over low heat on the stovetop or in the oven. Braised foods are moist, tender and richly flavored.

Marinating

Most of the recipes in this book involve the use of a marinade—one of the cornerstones of Chinese cooking. Marinades vary from one recipe to the next, and serve a variety of purposes. They can add flavor, tenderize, and seal in the flavor of foods. Common marinade ingredients include soy sauce, salt, wine, white pepper and cornstarch.

Soaking

This not only refers to what the chef does in a hot tub after cooking all day. It's also a prep technique used to soften certain dried ingredients (including black mushrooms, dried noodles, tangerine peel and dried shrimp) before cooking them.

Dried Mushrooms. To soak dried mushrooms (such as "black" or *shiitake* mushrooms) or black fungus (such as "cloud ears" or "wood ears"), place them in a small bowl and cover them with water. Let them stand about 15 minutes. Remove them carefully, allowing any grit to settle to the bottom of the soaking water, then rinse them under water to remove residual grit. Trim away and discard tough, fibrous stems with kitchen shears or a paring knife. If desired, you can strain the soaking liquid from black mushrooms through a coffee filter and reserve it to enrich broths and sauces.

Noodles. Dried bean thread and rice noodles often need to be softened in water before you add them to a soup or stir-fry dish. Soak them in plenty of water for about 10 minutes. Remember, they absorb a surprising amount of water.

Making Perfect Chinese Rice

Here's my foolproof formula for making long-grain rice that's flavorful and fluffy — like the kind you're used to eating in Chinese restaurants — on the stovetop. (If you have an electric rice cooker, follow the manufacturer's directions.) For three cups of cooked rice, start with one cup of raw, long-grain rice. Place it in a medium saucepan with 1½ cups cold water and bring it to a boil over medium-high heat. Boil, uncovered, for 10 minutes or until the water has evaporated and small holes appear in the surface of the rice. Reduce heat to low. Cover and simmer for 18 to 20 minutes or until the rice is tender. Remove from heat and let stand, covered, 5 minutes longer. Fluff the rice with a fork; it will be perfect every time.

THE CHINESE PANTRY

Keeping a well-stocked larder of Chinese dry goods and refrigerated and frozen ingredients will enable you to whip up an authentic Chinese meal on short notice. Stock up on the items below, and all you'll need to buy are a few fresh ingredients to make most of the recipes in this book.

Canned Goods
- Bamboo shoots
- Broth (beef, chicken or vegetable)
- Coconut milk
- Lychee
- Mandarin oranges
- Mushrooms, straw
- Water chestnuts

Dry Goods
- Black beans, salted
- Chinese Shao Hsing wine
- Cloud ear (fungus)
- Cornstarch
- Ginger, candied
- Mushrooms, black
- Nuts (walnuts, cashews)
- Rice, long-grain
- Sesame seeds

Noodles
- Bean thread noodles
- Egg noodles, fresh (store in freezer)
- Rice stick noodles

Oils
- Chili oil
- Cooking oil
- Sesame oil

Sauces & Condiments
- Black bean sauce
- Chili garlic sauce
- Hoisin sauce
- Oyster-flavored sauce
- Plum sauce
- Rice vinegar
- Soy sauce (light, dark or reduced-sodium)
- Sweet and sour sauce

Spices & Seasonings
- Crushed red pepper
- Dried tangerine peel
- Five-spice powder
- Mustard powder
- Sichuan peppercorns, toasted and ground
- Star anise
- White pepper

Wrappers
(store in freezer)
- Egg roll or Spring roll wrappers
- Wonton

Don't eat to live, live to eat.

"Don't eat to live, live to eat" is my all-time favorite Chinese saying. Cooking is one of the great joys of life. And my culinary journey through China was an important reminder to me about the things in life that really matter: goodwill, good friends, good health, good food and good fun. I hope this book adds a little more of each to your life. Now, as my mom would say, "Enough talking. Let's eat!"

Beijing~Cuisine

My Culinary journey began in Beijing (Peking), the "Northern Capital" that has been the center of Chinese culture, commerce and government for much of China's history. As the seat of the imperial court, Beijing attracted the greatest chefs in the land, and its cuisine combines the best of many regions, most notably neighboring Shandong and Mongolia. Harsh winters and cold northern winds make this area

# of Emperors

unsuitable for growing rice, so the staple crops are wheat, soybeans, and other grains, which find their way to the table in a variety of breads, dumplings and noodles. Aromatic roots and vegetables, such as garlic, leeks, ginger, onions, peppers and cabbage are used frequently, and this is the part of China where you're most likely to find beef, lamb and pork.

A classic street food of Northern China, these flaky breads are traditionally stuffed with slices of roasted lamb (page 81). I think of them as the Chinese answer to puff pastry. Instead of layering butter into the dough as the French do, Chinese bakers use a roux made from oil and flour.

SESAME SEED PILLOWS

SEEDS OF SUCCESS

What's black and white and used all over China? Sesame seeds! The white variety are sweet and nutty, while black seeds (which simply come from a different kind of sesame plant) have a slightly bitter taste. Both are much cheaper when bought in bulk at Asian markets. Toast them over medium heat in an ungreased skillet for a few minutes to bring out their flavor, and keep them on hand for a quick garnish.

Roux
¼ cup cooking oil
½ cup all-purpose flour

2½ cups all-purpose flour
¾ cup boiling water
¼ cup cold water
¾ teaspoon salt
¼ cup white sesame seeds
2 teaspoons black sesame seeds

Method
1. Prepare roux: Place a small heavy saucepan over medium-high heat until hot. Add oil, swirling to coat sides. Add flour and cook, stirring, until mixture turns golden brown. Let cool.

2. Place flour in a bowl. Add boiling water, stirring with chopsticks or a fork. Gradually stir in cold water, mixing until dough holds together. On a lightly floured board, knead dough until smooth and satiny, about 5 minutes. Cover and let rest for 30 minutes.

3. On a lightly floured board, roll dough into a 10-inch by 16-inch rectangle. Spread cooled roux over dough; sprinkle with salt. Fold dough into thirds; pinch edges to seal. Roll dough again into a 10-inch by 16-inch rectangle and repeat folding and pinching once. Turn dough 90° and repeat rolling, folding, and pinching once. Turn dough 90° again and repeat rolling, folding, and pinching once. Roll dough into a 10-inch by 16-inch rectangle one last time. Roll dough into a cylinder, then cut into 16 portions.

4. Combine white and black sesame seeds on a plate. To make each pillow, roll each portion of dough into a 2-inch by 3½-inch rectangle; keep remaining dough covered to prevent drying. Place dough in sesame seed mixture and lightly press to coat one side. Place on an ungreased baking sheet, seed side up, and let pillows rest for at least 5 minutes before baking.

5. Preheat oven to 375°F. Bake pillows until golden brown, 25 to 35 minutes. Serve hot.

Makes 16

Potstickers are one of the most famous specialties of Beijing's curbside restaurants. These can be prepared ahead and frozen. If you can't find potsticker wrappers, buy wonton skins and use a round biscuit cutter or scissors to make circular wrappers.

POTSTICKERS

Filling
6 dried black mushrooms
1 cup sliced regular cabbage
¼ teaspoon salt
½ pound lean ground chicken, pork, or beef
2 cups sliced napa cabbage
3 green onions, chopped
1 tablespoon minced ginger
⅓ cup chicken broth
1 tablespoon soy sauce
1 tablespoon cornstarch
½ teaspoon sugar
½ teaspoon white pepper
1 Chinese sausage (about 2 ounces), chopped

24 potsticker or gyoza wrappers
3 tablespoons cooking oil
⅔ cup chicken broth
Chili oil and rice vinegar

Method
1. Soak mushrooms in warm water to cover until softened, about 15 minutes; drain. Trim and discard stems. Finely chop caps. Combine regular cabbage and salt in a bowl; let stand for 15 minutes. Squeeze to remove excess liquid. Place mushrooms, cabbage, and remaining filling ingredients in a bowl; mix well.

2. Place a frying pan over high heat until hot. Add Chinese sausage and cook until fat is rendered, about 1 minute. Remove and drain on paper towels. Add to filling and mix well.

3. To fill each potsticker, place a heaping teaspoon of filling in center of a potsticker wrapper; keep remaining wrappers covered to prevent drying. Brush edges of wrapper with water and fold wrapper in half, crimping one side, to form a semi-circle. Pinch edges to seal. Set potsticker down on a baking sheet, seem side up, so that potsticker will sit flat. Cover filled potstickers with a dry towel.

4. Place a wide frying pan over medium heat until hot. Add 1½ tablespoons cooking oil, swirling to coat sides. Add potstickers, half at a time, seam side up. Cook until bottoms are golden brown, 3 to 4 minutes. Add ⅓ cup broth; reduce heat to low, cover, and cook until liquid is absorbed, 5 to 6 minutes.

5. Place potstickers, browned side up, on a serving plate with chili oil and rice vinegar on the side.

Makes 24

MAKING POTSTICKERS

Place filling in center of wrapper.

Fold over, crimping one side.

Cook seam-side up.

These unleavened fried breads are thin and flat, crispy on the outside, moist and chewy inside and bursting with oniony flavor. I like to serve them the traditional way, as the street vendors do: sliced in wedges and eaten out of hand, plain or with a spicy chili-garlic dipping sauce.

GREEN ONION CAKES

STREET TREATS

While filming in Beijing, our crew developed a serious addiction to green onion cakes, pan-fried in oil over a coal burner, from a certain tiny stall in Beijing's sprawling Wong Fu Jin night market where fast-food was invented. We went back night after night to feast on regional specialties like crispy spring rolls, potstickers, breads, pancakes, dumplings of every kind and steaming bowls of noodles. What fun! And what a bargain: a great meal with a beer and a view costs less than a dollar!

Dough
3⅓ cups all-purpose flour
1¼ cups warm water
¼ cup shortening or cooking oil
2 teaspoons sesame oil
1 cup chopped green onions
2 teaspoons salt
½ teaspoon white pepper

Dipping Sauce
½ cup chicken broth
2 tablespoons soy sauce
2 teaspoons chopped green onions
1 teaspoon minced garlic
1 teaspoon chili sauce

Cooking oil for pan-frying

Method
1. Place flour in a bowl. Add water, stirring with chopsticks or a fork, until dough holds together. On a lightly floured board, knead dough until smooth and satiny, about 5 minutes. Cover and let rest for 30 minutes.

2. Combine dipping sauce ingredients in a bowl; set aside.

3. On a lightly floured board, roll dough into a cylinder, then cut into 12 portions. To make each cake, roll a portion of dough to make an 8-inch circle about ⅛-inch thick; keep remaining dough covered to prevent drying. Brush with shortening. Sprinkle sesame oil, green onions, salt, and pepper on top. Roll dough into a cylinder and coil dough into a round patty; tuck end of dough underneath. Roll again to make an 8-inch circle about ⅛-inch thick.

4. Place a 10-inch frying pan over medium heat. Add 2 tablespoons oil, swirling to coat sides. Add a cake and cook until golden brown on each side, 2 to 3 minutes on each side. Remove and drain on paper towels. Add more oil as needed, swirling to coat sides. Repeat with remaining cakes.

5. Cut cakes into wedges and serve hot with dipping sauce on the side.

Makes 12

Coated with crunchy walnuts and sesame seeds, these golden chicken nuggets make great party food. You can shape and coat them several hours in advance and store them in the refrigerator, but wait until the last minute to deep-fry them.

CHICKEN-WALNUT CROQUETTES

FOWL MEMORIES

When I was a kid in Guangzhou, a crowing rooster woke me up every morning, and we always had a few chickens scratching around the yard. My mom had a remarkable talent for turning a single chicken into several meals and using every last bit for soup stock, home remedies and medicinal poultices. The sound of chickens clucking always makes me think of China, where chickens are a universal delicacy: even the poorest families will raise their own for an occasional special meal.

¾ **pound boneless, skinless chicken**

Marinade
1 egg white, lightly beaten
1 tablespoon rice wine
    or dry sherry
1 tablespoon cornstarch
¾ **teaspoon salt**
¼ **teaspoon white pepper**

¾ **cup finely chopped**
    toasted walnuts
⅓ **cup toasted sesame seeds**
1 sheet Japanese seaweed *(nori)*
Cooking oil for deep-frying
Prepared sweet and sour sauce

Method

1. Cut chicken into 1-inch pieces. Place chicken in a food processor and coarsely chop. Combine marinade ingredients in a bowl. Add chicken and mix well. Let stand for 10 minutes.

2. Combine walnuts and sesame seeds on a plate. Cut seaweed into 12 strips, each about ¾-inch wide.

3. Divide chicken mixture into 12 portions. With wet hands, roll each portion into a cylinder about 4-inches long and 1-inch wide. Roll each croquette in the walnut mixture, lightly press to coat. Wrap a strip of seaweed around the middle; brush edges with water and press to seal.

4. Heat oil in a wok to 350°F. Deep-fry croquettes, a few at a time, and cook, turning frequently, until golden brown on all sides, about 4 minutes. Remove and drain on paper towels.

5. Serve hot with sweet and sour sauce.

Makes 4 to 6 servings

The secret to these crispy-fried wings is their coating of Japanese-style "panko" breadcrumbs, which have a wonderfully crunchy texture. If you can't find panko, use ordinary breadcrumbs, or make your own from stale crusty bread.

BEIJING WINGS

8 chicken wings

<u>Marinade</u>
2 tablespoons soy sauce
2 tablespoons rice wine or
 dry sherry
1 tablespoon cornstarch
¼ teaspoon Chinese five-spice
¼ teaspoon ground toasted Sichuan
 peppercorns
⅛ teaspoon white pepper

¼ cup cornstarch
¼ cup panko (Japanese-style
 breadcrumbs)
2 teaspoons toasted sesame seeds
1 egg white, lightly beaten
Cooking oil for pan-frying
Pepper Salt (see page 109)

<u>Method</u>
1. Cut chicken wings into sections; save wing tips for other uses. Combine marinade ingredients in a bowl. Add chicken wings and stir to coat. Let stand for 10 minutes.

2. Combine cornstarch, panko, and sesame seeds in a bowl; set aside.

3. Place a wok or wide frying pan over medium-high heat. Add oil to a depth of ¼-inch. Dip chicken wings in egg white, drain briefly, then dredge in cornstarch mixture. Shake to remove excess. Add chicken wings and pan-fry, covered, turning once, until meat near bone is no longer pink and chicken wings are golden brown, 5 to 6 minutes. Remove and drain on paper towels.

4. Serve hot with Pepper Salt on the side.

Makes 16

A WING & A PRAYER
Chickens hold a special place in Chinese ritual and symbology. They were used as sacrificial offerings in ancient China, and were thought to possess life-giving powers. The rooster gets a place of honor in the Chinese zodiac, too, and its crowing is credited with driving away the evil spirits of the night. Black chickens (whose skin and bones are naturally dark black) are not only wonderfully juicy and flavorful, they're also believed to restore youthful vigor and good looks. I'm keeping my fingers crossed!

In Beijing's Nan May street market, you can buy all kinds of chickens, including exotic black ones.

47

Northern Chinese-style "ravioli" make an unusual first course. You can also deep-fry these and serve them as finger food with the Hot and Sour Sauce or prepared Sweet and Sour Sauce on the side for dipping.

HOT AND SOUR BEIJING DUMPLINGS

HERE'S THE WRAP

What's the difference between all those wrappers on the market? Most are made of egg noodle dough (flour, water and a small amount of egg), the main difference being their shape and thickness. Wonton wrappers—and their larger cousins, egg roll wrappers, are square. Potsticker wrappers—also sold as Japanese *gyoza* wrappers—are round. Spring roll wrappers, made without the egg, are paper thin and delicately crisp when fried.

Filling
¼ pound lean ground beef, chicken, or pork
¼ pound raw shrimp, shelled, deveined, and chopped
1 green onion, chopped
1 tablespoon oyster flavored sauce
2 teaspoons cornstarch
¼ teaspoon black pepper
⅛ teaspoon salt

16 to 18 wonton wrappers

Sauce
¼ cup ketchup
¼ cup chicken broth
3 tablespoons rice vinegar
1 teaspoon sesame oil
2 teaspoons chili garlic sauce
1 tablespoon sugar
2 teaspoons cornstarch
¼ teaspoon white pepper

Cilantro sprigs or chopped green onion for garnish

Method
1. Combine filling ingredients in a bowl; mix well.

2. To fill each dumpling, place a heaping teaspoon of filling in center of a wonton wrapper; keep remaining wrappers covered to prevent drying. Brush edges of wrapper with water and fold wrapper in half to form a triangle. Pinch edges to seal. Cover filled dumplings with a dry towel.

3. Bring a pot of water to a boil. Add dumplings and cook until they float to the top, 2 to 3 minutes. Drain, rinse with cold water, and drain again.

4. Combine sauce ingredients in a saucepan. Heat sauce over medium heat and cook, stirring, until sauce boils and thickens.

5. Divide dumplings among 4 plates or in 4 shallow bowls. Pour sauce over dumplings and garnish with a cilantro sprig.

Makes 4 servings

Egg roll wrappers, potsticker (gyoza) wrappers, wonton wrappers.

Originally a Shanghai specialty, spring rolls are served in many parts of China on the first day of spring, which is also the Chinese New Year. Here's an easy way to miniaturize them for a year-round appetizer.

MINIATURE SPRING ROLLS

FOLDING SPRING ROLLS

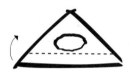

Fold bottom of wrapper over filling.

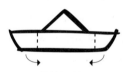

Fold in sides.

Roll up to enclose filling.

Cook and eat!

Filling
3 dried black mushrooms
2 ounces dried bean thread noodles
    or dried rice stick noodles
1 small carrot, julienned
1 cup thinly sliced napa cabbage
3 green onions, sliced

½ pound boneless chicken or pork

Marinade
2 tablespoons chicken broth
1 tablespoon oyster flavored sauce
½ teaspoon sesame oil
2 teaspoons cornstarch
¼ teaspoon Chinese five-spice

1 tablespoon cooking oil
12 spring roll or egg roll wrappers,
    cut in half diagonally
Cooking oil for deep-frying

Method
1. Soak mushrooms in warm water to cover until softened, about 15 minutes; drain. Trim stems and thinly slice caps. Soak bean threads in warm water to cover until softened, about 15 minutes; drain. Cut bean thread noodles into 4-inch lengths. Combine mushrooms and bean thread noodles in a bowl and add remaining filling ingredients; mix well.

2. Cut chicken into thin slices then cut slices into thin strips. Combine marinade ingredients in a bowl. Add chicken and stir to coat. Let stand for 10 minutes.

3. Place a wok over high heat until hot. Add 1 tablespoon oil, swirling to coat sides. Add chicken and stir-fry for 1½ minutes. Add filling ingredients and stir-fry for 30 seconds. Remove the chicken mixture to a bowl and let cool.

4. To make each spring roll, place a triangular wrapper on work surface with long side facing you; keep remaining wrappers covered to prevent drying. Place 2 tablespoons filling in a band along base of wrapper. Fold bottom over filling, then fold in left and right sides. Brush edges with water and roll up to completely enclose filling.

5. Heat oil in a wok to 360°F. Deep-fry spring rolls, a few at a time, and cook, turning occasionally, until golden brown, about 3 minutes. Remove and drain on paper towels.

Makes 24

These delicate meat-filled dumplings are first pan-fried, then steamed in water or broth in the style of potstickers. For a lighter presentation, cook them in a steamer over boiling water (as shown at left).

FLOWER PETAL DUMPLINGS

Filling
2 dried black mushrooms
¼ pound napa cabbage, finely chopped
½ pound lean ground chicken, pork, or beef
1 tablespoon chopped green onions
2 teaspoons minced ginger
2 tablespoons oyster flavored sauce
1 teaspoon sesame oil
¼ teaspoon white pepper

18 gyoza, potsticker, or wonton wrappers
2 tablespoons frozen peas, thawed
3 tablespoons cooking oil
⅔ cup chicken broth
Soy sauce, chili oil, and rice vinegar for dipping

Method
1. Prepare filling: Soak mushrooms in warm water to cover until softened, about 15 minutes; drain. Trim and discard stems. Finely chop caps. Place cabbage in a clean towel and squeeze to remove excess water. Combine mushrooms and cabbage in a bowl and add remaining filling ingredients; mix well.

2. If using wonton wrappers, cut them into circles with a biscuit cutter. To fill each dumpling, place a heaping teaspoon of filling in center of a wrapper; keep remaining wrappers covered to prevent drying. Fold wrapper in half to form a semi-circle; pinch center to seal. Bring opposite sides of wrapper together and pinch to seal so the top starts to form petals. Line up edges and pinch to seal. Place a pea on top for garnish. Cover filled dumplings with a dry towel.

3. Place a wide frying pan over medium heat until hot. Add 1½ tablespoons cooking oil, swirling to coat sides. Add dumplings, half at a time, seam side up. Cook until bottoms are golden brown, 3 to 4 minutes. Add ⅓ cup broth; reduce heat to low, cover, and cook until liquid is absorbed, 5 to 6 minutes.

4. Place dumplings on a serving plate with soy sauce, chili oil, and vinegar on the side.

Makes 18

DUMPLING TIPS
Keep wonton or other wrappers covered with a towel as you work so they don't dry out. Place filled dumplings on a plate dusted with a little cornstarch to keep them from sticking to the plate. I like to make extra dumplings. I freeze them in a single layer on a baking sheet until firm, then transfer them to a plastic container or freezer bag. Cook frozen dumplings without thawing, adding 3 to 4 minutes to the cooking time.

Flower Petal Dumplings in steamer

Talk about a quick way to make some dough! Round, golden and full of flavor, these pan-fried dumplings with a rich meat filling symbolize wholeness and good fortune.

GOLDEN MEAT-FILLED COINS

POTS OF GOLD

When it comes to cooking, the Chinese know how to put their money where their mouth is. Many dishes are either named after or symbolic of gold, coins or money—and eating them is believed to bring prosperity. Nowhere is this symbolism more pronounced than during the New Year celebration, in dishes like Red Envelope Fish (referring to the envelopes in which New Year *lai see* money is given), and Spring Rolls, designed to evoke tiny bars of gold.

2¼ cups all-purpose flour
½ cup boiling water
⅓ cup cold water

Filling
½ pound lean ground chicken, beef, or pork
3 tablespoons chopped green onions
1 tablespoon minced ginger
¼ cup chicken broth
1 tablespoon soy sauce
1 tablespoon oyster flavored sauce
2 teaspoons sesame oil
½ teaspoon sugar
¼ teaspoon white pepper

4 tablespoons cooking oil

Method
1. Place flour in a bowl. Add boiling water, stirring with chopsticks or a fork. Gradually stir in cold water, mixing until dough holds together. On a lightly floured board, knead dough until smooth and satiny, about 5 minutes. Cover and let rest for 30 minutes.

2. Combine filling ingredients in a bowl; mix well.

3. On a lightly floured board, roll dough into a cylinder, then cut into 18 portions. To make each coin, roll a portion of dough into a 3½-inch circle about ½-inch thick; keep remaining dough covered to prevent drying.

4. Place a rounded tablespoon of filling in center of dough. Gather edges of dough around filling; pinch to seal. Roll filled dough into a ball; flatten with the palm of your hand until ½-inch thick.

5. Place a wide frying pan over medium heat until hot. Add 2 tablespoons oil, swirling to coat sides. Add coins, half at a time, and cook until golden brown on both sides, 3 to 4 minutes on each side.

Makes 18

M y Uncle Lu has a bowl of noodle soup almost every afternoon at the counter of a storefront on Long Fung Ar Tiau Street. Here's a quick Beijing-style noodle soup I wouldn't mind eating every day.

BEIJING NOODLE SOUP

4 dried black mushrooms
¼ pound medium raw shrimp,
shelled and deveined

Marinade
1 tablespoon soy sauce
1 teaspoon rice wine or dry sherry
1 teaspoon cornstarch

1 package (about 12 ounces)
fresh Chinese egg noodles
5 cups chicken broth
2 ounces tender boneless beef,
chicken, or pork, thinly sliced
¼ pound napa cabbage or regular
cabbage, sliced
2 tablespoons oyster flavored sauce
1 teaspoon chili garlic sauce
1 teaspoon sesame oil
Thinly sliced Japanese seaweed
(*nori*) for garnish

Method
1. Soak mushrooms in warm water to cover until softened, about 15 minutes; drain. Trim and discard stems. Thinly slice caps. Cut shrimp in half horizontally. Combine marinade ingredients in a bowl. Add shrimp and stir to coat. Let stand for 10 minutes.

2. Cook noodles in a pot of boiling water according to package directions. Drain, rinse with cold water, and drain again.

3. Place broth in a 2-quart pot; bring to a boil. Add beef, mushrooms, and cabbage. Reduce heat to low, cover, and simmer for 3 minutes. Add shrimp and simmer for 1 minute. Add noodles, oyster flavored sauce, chili garlic sauce, and sesame oil; cook until heated through. Ladle into individual bowls and garnish with seaweed.

Makes 4
servings

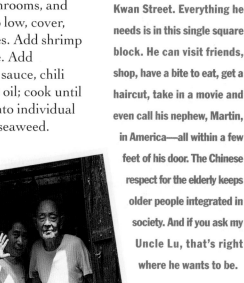

UNCLE LU

When I'm old, I hope I'm as content as my Uncle Lu. He's 86, and he lives in a tiny room on Beijing's crowded Mun Kwan Street. Everything he needs is in this single square block. He can visit friends, shop, have a bite to eat, get a haircut, take in a movie and even call his nephew, Martin, in America—all within a few feet of his door. The Chinese respect for the elderly keeps older people integrated in society. And if you ask my Uncle Lu, that's right where he wants to be.

$\mathcal{W}$hile in Beijing, I ate at the world-famous Hui Zhen Restaurant, where Peking Duck is the specialty of the house, and no duck dinner is complete without a simple soup made from the carcass.

DUCK SOUP

5 cups chicken broth
1 carcass from a roast duck
2 slices ginger, lightly crushed
2 green onions, cut into 2-inch
    pieces

2 dried black mushrooms
1 package (16 ounces) soft tofu,
    drained
2 cups sliced napa cabbage
½ cup sliced bamboo shoots
½ cup shredded roast duck meat
1 tablespoon soy sauce
2 teaspoons rice wine or dry sherry

Method

1. Place broth, duck carcass, ginger, and green onions in a large pot; bring to a boil. Reduce heat to low, cover, and simmer for 2 hours. Strain broth and discard solids. Return broth to the pot and continue simmering over low heat.

2. Soak mushrooms in warm water to cover until softened, about 15 minutes; drain. Trim and discard stems. Thinly slice caps. Cut tofu into ½-inch cubes.

3. Add mushrooms, cabbage, and bamboo shoots to broth; cook until cabbage is tender, 4 to 5 minutes. Add tofu, duck meat, soy sauce, and wine; cook until heated through.

Makes 4 to 6 servings

QUACK MEDICINE?

The Chinese believe that if you slaughter an animal, no edible part should be wasted. Not a bad idea when you have 1.2 billion mouths to feed! It's common practice to use the carcass of a duck to make a light soup, served at the end of the meal as a digestive. Duck soup has other amazing powers, too. Ancient Chinese pharmacologists routinely prescribed it to couples who were having marital difficulties!

We found these healthful vegetarian rolls in Beijing's Wong Fu Jin Market at a stand run by a family from Shandong Province. If you're using tortillas or spring roll wrappers, wrap a few at a time in a damp towel and steam them in a bamboo steamer for 5 minutes before rolling.

CHILLED VEGETABLE ROLL WITH THIN PANCAKE

EAT YOUR VEGGIES

"Eat your vegetables" is a phrase few Chinese mothers ever utter to their children. And not just because it's in English! You learn to love vegetables from an early age in China because along with rice and, in the North, breads, they're really what most every-day meals are made of—and they're really wonderful! When you prepare vegetables as the Chinese do, with great respect for their integrity, flavor and nutrients, they become the main event of a meal, not just a second-class side dish.

4 dried black mushrooms
6 pieces dried cloud ear
2 ounces dried bean thread noodles
1 tablespoon cooking oil
1 teaspoon minced garlic
1 cup thinly sliced cabbage
¼ cup julienned carrots
½ cup chicken broth
1 cup fresh mung bean sprouts
1½ cups egg shreds (see page 190)
2 tablespoons oyster flavored sauce
2 teaspoons sugar
2 teaspoons sesame oil
Hoisin sauce
Cilantro sprigs
Spring roll wrappers, Mandarin pancakes, rice papers, or flour tortillas

Method

1. Soak mushrooms and cloud ears in warm water to cover until softened, about 15 minutes; drain. Trim and discard stems. Thinly slice mushroom caps and cloud ears. Soak bean thread noodles in warm water to cover until softened, about 15 minutes; drain. Cut bean thread noodles into 4-inch lengths.

2. Place a wok over high heat until hot. Add cooking oil, swirling to coat sides. Add garlic and cook, stirring, until fragrant, about 10 seconds. Add mushrooms, cloud ears, cabbage, and carrots; stir-fry for 30 seconds. Add bean thread noodles and broth; cook for 2 minutes.

3. Add mung bean sprouts, egg shreds, oyster flavored sauce, sugar, and sesame oil; cook until heated through. Remove to a serving bowl and serve hot or let cool, cover, and refrigerate until chilled.

4. To eat, spread hoisin sauce on a steamed spring roll wrapper, spoon in some of vegetable mixture, top with cilantro sprigs, roll up, and eat out of hand.

Makes 4 to 6 servings

This simple vegetarian dish was inspired by a meal we were served at the Shaolin Monastery. When you marinate and lightly fry tofu before braising, it takes on a golden color, a slightly crispy texture and a rich, meaty flavor.

BRAISED VEGETABLE-TOFU CASSEROLE

6 dried black mushrooms
½ package (7 ounces) regular-firm
    tofu, drained
2 teaspoons soy sauce
1 tablespoon cornstarch
2 tablespoons cooking oil
1 small zucchini, sliced
½ cup sliced bamboo shoots
1 leek (white part only), cut into
    ½-inch rings
¾ cup vegetable broth
2 tablespoons soy sauce
2 teaspoons sugar
1 teaspoon sesame oil
1 teaspoon cornstarch dissolved
    in 2 teaspoons water (optional)

Method

1. Soak mushrooms in warm water to cover until softened, about 15 minutes; drain. Trim and discard stems. Leave caps whole. Cut tofu into ¾-inch cubes. Place tofu in a bowl with soy sauce and stir gently to coat. Sprinkle cornstarch over tofu then stir to coat all sides.

2. Place a wide non-stick frying pan over medium heat until hot. Add 1 tablespoon cooking oil, swirling to coat sides. Add tofu and cook until golden brown on all sides, about 3 minutes. Remove and drain on paper towels.

3. Place a wok over high heat until hot. Add remaining 1 tablespoon cooking oil, swirling to coat sides. Add mushrooms, zucchini, bamboo shoots, leeks; stir-fry for 2 minutes. Add a few drops of water if wok appears dry. Add tofu and cook for 1 minute.

4. Place vegetable mixture in a clay pot or 2-quart pot. Add broth, soy sauce, sugar, and sesame oil; bring to a boil over medium heat. Reduce heat to low, cover, and simmer until vegetables are tender, 6 to 8 minutes. If desired, add cornstarch solution and cook, stirring, until sauce boils and thickens.

Makes 4 servings

YAN CAN KICK

Shaolin Temple in Henan Province is a 1,500-year-old Buddhist monastery that is the world's most revered center of *wushu*, or martial arts. Its school attracts thousands of young devotees from all over the world each year. As a kid, I practiced Kung Fu every day and I always dreamt of studying at Shaolin. That dream finally came true, when the monks bestowed on me the great honor of inviting me to put on their saffron robes and join in their sunrise training.

When I was growing up, we often made a light meal of an omelet, served in the Chinese home-style way: simply seasoned, then cooked open-faced, cut into wedges and topped with a tangy vegetable sauce.

OPEN-FACE OMELET WITH SAVORY GARLIC SAUCE

YIN, YANG & YOLK

To the Chinese, the egg is more than a versatile food. It's an important cultural symbol, thought to embody not only the beginning of the life cycle, but also the wholeness of yin (the white, representing bright, male energy and heaven) and yang (the yolk, repre-senting dark, female energy and earth) held together in a circle (the shell, rep-resenting creation). The joining of yin and yang cre-ates a balance of wisdom, truth, purity, propriety and kindness, making the egg the "food of five virtues."

4 eggs, lightly beaten
¼ teaspoon salt
⅛ teaspoon white pepper
2 teaspoons chopped green onion

Sauce
⅓ cup vegetable broth
2 tablespoons soy sauce
1 tablespoon black vinegar
    or balsamic vinegar
2 teaspoons chili garlic sauce
1 teaspoon sesame oil
2 teaspoons sugar

1 ½ tablespoons cooking oil
1 teaspoon minced garlic
1 teaspoon minced ginger
½ cup diced tomatoes
½ cup chopped water chestnuts
¼ cup frozen peas, thawed
1 teaspoon cornstarch dissolved
    in 2 teaspoons water

Method
1. Combine eggs, salt, pepper, and green onion in a bowl. Combine sauce ingredients in another bowl; set aside.

2. Place an 8 or 9-inch non-stick omelet pan over medium heat until hot. Add 1 tablespoon oil, swirling to coat sides. Add eggs and cook without stirring. As edges begin to set, lift with a spatula and shake or tilt to let egg flow underneath. When egg no longer flows freely, turn omelet over and brown lightly on the other side. Slide omelet onto a warm serving plate. Cut into 6 to 8 wedges.

3. Place a saucepan over high heat until hot. Add remaining ½ tablespoon oil, swirling to coat sides. Add garlic and ginger; cook, stirring, until fra-grant, about 10 seconds. Add tomatoes, water chestnuts, peas, and sauce; bring to a boil. Add cornstarch solution and cook, stirring, until sauce boils and thickens. Pour over omelet and serve.

Makes 4 servings

If you're looking for authentic Chinese comfort food, look no further. The time-honored method of steaming eggs produces a custard of delicate texture, so light you can eat it any time of day. Steam the eggs slowly over medium heat to keep them smooth and soft. The custard is ready to eat the moment a knife inserted in the center comes out clean.

STEAMED VELVET EGG CUSTARD

EGGS ANY STYLE

In China, eggs go way beyond hard-boiled. "Thousand year old eggs" (really only about 100 days old) are coated with a mixture of clay, lime, salt, tea and bits of straw, which cures and "cooks" the egg, turning it into a dark green gelatinous delicacy that's an acquired taste for most westerners. Marble eggs, sold by street vendors and eaten as between-act snacks at the Chinese opera, are first boiled, then steeped in a spicy tea mixture, giving them a beautiful marbled appearance. Scarlet eggs are dyed bright red and used as birth announcements—a basket of 8 or 10 eggs means it's a girl; 9 or 11 means it's a boy.

¼ **pound shelled raw shrimp, diced**
2 **tablespoons coarsely chopped Smithfield ham**
1 **teaspoon salt**
¼ **teaspoon white pepper**
4 **eggs, lightly beaten**
1 ¼ **cups water**
1 **tablespoon chopped green onion**

Method

1. Combine shrimp, ham, salt, and white pepper in a bowl; mix well. Combine egg and water in another bowl.

2. Pour both shrimp mixture and egg mixture into a heat-proof glass pie dish.

3. Prepare a wok for steaming (see page 29). Cover the dish with another heat-proof glass pie dish, place in the wok, cover, and steam for 15 minutes. Garnish with chopped green onion.

Stuffed cabbage, Peking-style: steamed napa cabbage rolls with a filling of tofu, brightened with carrots and mushrooms. For an elegant presentation, cut each roll on a slight diagonal and place one half lying down and the other standing on end.

PEKING CABBAGE PILLOWS

2 dried black mushrooms
6 large napa cabbage leaves
½ package (7 ounces) extra-firm
   tofu, drained
¼ cup chopped carrots
4 teaspoons cornstarch
2 tablespoons oyster-flavored sauce
2 teaspoons rice wine or dry sherry
1 teaspoon sesame oil
1 teaspoon minced ginger
1 teaspoon chopped cilantro

Sauce
⅓ cup chicken broth
2 teaspoons cornstarch
1 teaspoon sugar
¾ teaspoon salt

Method
1. Soak mushrooms in warm water to cover until softened, about 15 minutes; drain. Trim and discard stems. Dice caps.

2. Parboil cabbage in a pot of boiling water until limp, 2 to 3 minutes. Drain, rinse with cold water, and drain again. With a knife, shave thick ribs at stem ends to make leaves easier to roll.

3. Mash tofu in a bowl. Place tofu in a clean towel and squeeze to extract liquid. Return to bowl and add mushrooms, carrots, cornstarch, oyster flavored sauce, wine, sesame oil, ginger, and cilantro; mix well.

4. Place leaves, trimmed side up, on work surface. To stuff each leaf, mound about 2 tablespoons tofu mixture at base of leaf; fold in lower edges, then sides, and roll to enclose. Place cabbage rolls, seam side down, without crowding, in a heat-proof glass pie dish.

5. Prepare a wok for steaming (see page 29). Cover and steam cabbage rolls over high heat for 10 minutes.

6. Combine sauce ingredients in a saucepan and cook, stirring, until sauce boils and thickens. Place cabbage rolls on a serving plate and pour sauce over the top.

Makes 6 servings

NAPA CABBAGE

Psst. There's something you need to know about napa cabbage: it has nothing to do with the Napa Valley, which, after all, is famous as California's wine country, not California's cabbage patch! Its name probably comes from the Japanese word *nappa*, meaning "greens." Now that we've cleared that up, what *is* napa cabbage? It's a pale green and yellow oblong cabbage also sold as Chinese or Tien Zhen cabbage. I love it in simple salads and stir-fries, and the broad outer leaves are great for stuffing and for lining your steamer basket.

I'm a big fan of vegetables. And this dish is a slightly smaller one. It's a charming banquet-style presentation that demonstrates a classic Chinese approach: start with a handful of simple vegetables, add a dash of flavor—in this case, curry—and a little imagination and you end up with a healthful, tasty work of art.

FOUR COLOR VEGETABLE FAN

7 dried black mushrooms
9 large asparagus spears

Sauce
½ cup vegetable broth
3 tablespoons prepared curry sauce
   or 1 ½ tablespoons curry powder
2 tablespoons rice wine
   or dry sherry
2 teaspoons sesame oil
2 teaspoons cornstarch

1 teaspoon salt
1 teaspoon cooking oil
6 to 8 large white button
   mushrooms
8 ears baby corn
1 green onion, bottom 5 inches only

Method
1. Soak black mushrooms in warm water to cover until softened, about 15 minutes; drain. Trim and discard stems. Leave caps whole. Trim asparagus so spears are the same length as baby corn. Combine sauce ingredients in a saucepan; set aside.

2. Bring a pot of water to a boil. Add salt, oil, all mushrooms, asparagus, and baby corn. Cook until asparagus is crisp-tender, 1 to 2 minutes. Add green onion and cook for 10 seconds. Drain, rinse with cold water, and drain again.

3. Arrange vegetables so they resemble a fan: Alternate asparagus and baby corn across top half of serving plate. Place black mushrooms at base of fan. Arrange button mushrooms below black mushrooms. Place green onion below mushrooms to form a handle.

4. Heat sauce over medium heat and cook, stirring, until sauce boils and thickens. Pour sauce over vegetables.

Makes 4 servings

Fish steamed in rice wine and rice wine "lees" (the fermented rice that's a byproduct of the rice wine making process) is a classic regional specialty of eastern and northern China. You can find fermented rice at Asian groceries, sold as a semi-liquid paste in jars. It imparts a wonderful yeasty flavor and a delicate rice wine aroma.

FISH FILLET IN WINE SAUCE

6 pieces dried cloud ear
1 ½ pounds firm white fish fillets,
    such as sea bass or red snapper,
    about ¼-inch thick
1 tablespoon cornstarch
¾ teaspoon salt
¼ teaspoon white pepper

<u>Wine Sauce</u>
⅓ cup rice wine or dry sherry
¼ cup chicken broth
1 tablespoon oyster flavored sauce
1 tablespoon regular soy sauce
1 teaspoon dark soy sauce
2 tablespoons fermented rice
    (optional)
1 teaspoon sugar

2 tablespoon cooking oil
½ cup sliced bamboo shoots
2 teaspoons cornstarch dissolved in
    1 tablespoon water (optional)

<u>Method</u>
1. Soak cloud ears in warm water to cover until softened, about 15 minutes; drain. Trim and discard stems. Thinly slice cloud ears.

2. Cut fish crosswise to make 2-inch by 4-inch pieces. Combine cornstarch, salt, and pepper in a bowl. Add fish and stir to coat. Let stand for 10 minutes. Combine sauce ingredients in a bowl; set aside.

3. Place a wide frying pan over high heat until hot. Add oil, swirling to coat sides. Add fish and cook, turning once, until fish turns opaque, about 1 ½ minutes on each side. Remove fish from pan.

4. Add bamboo shoots and cloud ears to pan; stir-fry for 1 minute. Return fish to pan and add sauce; bring to a boil. Reduce heat to low and simmer for 5 minutes. If desired, add cornstarch solution and cook, stirring, until sauce boils and thickens.

Makes 4 servings

PEDAL POWER

You seldom see overweight people in China. That's because the diet is quite healthy, people work like crazy and instead of driving, everyone rides a bike. In Beijing, a city of 11 million people, there are 11 million bicycles. Rush hour looks like the Tour de France! I grew up riding my dad's bike, and when I was going to school at the University of California at Davis, where bikes are far more popular than cars, I felt right at home. Besides being great exercise, bikes don't pollute and take up very little space. Imagine the kind of traffic jam you'd have if every one of the bikes in this picture were a car!

Fried fish topped with a cold fresh tomato sauce—this is my interpretation of a simple dish that my cousin threw together for dinner one warm night during my trip. I like the contrast of the crispy, golden fillets and the cool, sweet and slightly spicy "salsa."

FISH WITH SPICY SALSA

1 pound firm white fish fillets,
    such as sea bass or red snapper,
    each about ¾-inch thick

Marinade
2 teaspoons cornstarch
½ teaspoon salt
¼ teaspoon white pepper

Salsa
¼ cup diced tomatoes
¼ cup each diced red and green
    bell peppers
¼ cup chopped red onions
1 tablespoon chopped cilantro
3 tablespoons plum sauce
1 tablespoon seasoned rice vinegar
2 teaspoons soy sauce
1 teaspoon chili sauce

2 tablespoons cooking oil
Cornstarch for dry-coating

Method

1. Cut fish into serving size pieces. Combine marinade ingredients in a bowl. Add fish and stir to coat. Let stand for 10 minutes. Combine salsa ingredients in a bowl. Let stand for 10 minutes.

2. Place a wok or wide frying pan over medium-high heat until hot. Add oil, swirling to coat sides. Dredge fish in cornstarch; shake to remove excess.

3. Add fish and pan-fry, turning once, until golden brown, 3 to 4 minutes on each side. Remove and drain on paper towels.

4. Serve fish with salsa on the side.

Makes 4 servings

DOING THE TWIST

Whenever people ask me how I come up with recipes and ideas for new dishes, I always answer that my favorite Chinese cooking technique is one you can't find in any book: imagination. There's nothing more fun than taking a familiar idea and giving it a new twist. Take something you love to eat, and try changing a few ingredients. Say it's meatloaf. Why not add a little soy sauce instead of salt? How about cilantro instead of parsley? Throw in some water chestnuts for texture. Add some oyster sauce to the glaze on top. You get the idea: have fun and follow your nose!

A light touch is the key to preparing delicate ingredients like mushrooms and scallops. In this dish, they're cooked quickly to preserve their texture and served in a simple sauce that enhances their mild flavor without overpowering it.

BRAISED MUSHROOMS WITH SCALLOPS

STRAW MUSHROOMS

Canned straw mushrooms are widely available in the Asian sections of supermarkets. If you think canned mushrooms are boring, give straw mushrooms a try. True, their flavor is somewhat mild, but they have a wonderful meaty texture and a delightfully velvety feeling on the tongue. They're also cute to look at. With their tall, oblong caps and short bodies, they look like little cartoon characters that are just about to start dancing around and singing: "Hi ho, hi ho, it's off to wok we go!"

¾ pound sea scallops

Marinade
1 tablespoon cornstarch
½ teaspoon salt
¼ teaspoon white pepper

Sauce
⅓ cup chicken broth
2 tablespoons oyster flavored sauce
2 tablespoons rice wine
   or dry sherry
1 tablespoon dark soy sauce
½ teaspoon sesame oil

3 tablespoons cooking oil
2 teaspoons minced shallots
12 fresh shiitake mushrooms
   or oyster mushrooms
½ pound small white button
   mushrooms
1 cup straw mushrooms
2 teaspoons cornstarch dissolved
   in 1 tablespoon water

Method
1. Cut scallops in half horizontally. Combine marinade ingredients in a bowl. Add scallops and stir to coat. Let stand for 10 minutes. Combine sauce ingredients in a bowl; set aside.

2. Place a wok over high heat until hot. Add 2 tablespoons oil, swirling to coat sides. Add scallops and shallots; stir-fry until scallops turn opaque, about 1 minute. Remove the scallops from the wok.

3. Add remaining 1 tablespoon oil to wok, swirling to coat sides. Add all mushrooms and stir-fry for 1 minute. Add sauce and bring to a boil. Reduce heat to low, cover, and simmer for 5 minutes. Add cornstarch solution and cook, stirring, until sauce boils and thickens. Return scallops to wok and cook until heated through.

Makes 4 servings

Peeled and unpeeled straw mushrooms.

This is a fun one for tableside showmanship. You emerge from the kitchen and announce: "Butterflied Scallops!" Then you present this fanciful dish that actually looks like little butterflies. Applause guaranteed.

SCALLOP-TOFU BUTTERFLIES

8 dried black mushrooms
**1 package (16 ounces) soft tofu,
    drained**
8 sea scallops

Marinade
1 tablespoon cornstarch
¾ teaspoon salt
¼ teaspoon white pepper

1 sandwich-size sliced ham

Method
1. Soak mushrooms in warm water to cover until softened, about 15 minutes; drain. Trim and discard stems. Leave caps whole. Cut tofu in half horizontally to make 2 pieces, each about ¾-inch thick. Cut each half in to quarters to make a total of 8 rectangles.

2. Butterfly scallops. Combine marinade ingredients in a bowl. Add scallops and stir to coat. Let stand for 10 minutes. Cut ham to make 8 strips, each about ¾-inch wide and 2-inches long.

3. Place tofu in a heat-proof glass pie dish. Top each piece with a scallop. Center a mushroom on each scallop, then place a strip of ham across the middle of each mushroom so topping resembles a butterfly.

4. Prepare a wok for steaming (see page 29). Cover and steam over high heat until scallops turn opaque, 5 to 6 minutes. Transfer tofu to a serving plate with a slotted spatula and discard steaming liquid.

Makes 4 servings

WHAT SERVICE!
The Chinese love to invent beautiful and whimsical ways to serve food. Here are some easy tips:

• Prepare a simple garnish in advance—something edible that relates to the food and adds a little color to the plate.

• Choose serving dishes that complement the colors and shapes of the food.

• Vary the serving style: some dishes on individual plates or bowls, some on platters, some in unusual vessels, like a bamboo steamer.

• Name your creation, and present it with a flourish and, of course, a smile.

Seafood steamed in fresh orange cups with a little orange liqueur takes on a wonderfully perfumed flavor. Present these little "baskets" right in the steamer basket, then serve them on individual plates as an elegant first course.

SEAFOOD IN AN ORANGE BASKET

¼ **pound each crabmeat, sea scallops, and firm white fish fillet**

Marinade
2 tablespoons oyster flavored sauce
2 teaspoons cornstarch

4 navel oranges
2 teaspoons Grand Marnier
½ cup diced cantaloupe
⅓ cup diced water chestnuts
¼ cup frozen peas, thawed
1 tablespoon chopped crystallized ginger
3 tablespoons plum sauce
½ teaspoon sugar

Method

1. Cut crabmeat into ½-inch pieces. Combine marinade ingredients in a bowl. Add crabmeat, sea scallops, and fish fillet and stir to coat. Let stand for 10 minutes.

2. Prepare orange baskets: Remove a thin slice from bottom of each orange so it stands upright. Cut off top ⅓. With a small knife, score flesh into quarters, then remove flesh without tearing shell; reserve flesh. If you wish, notch the top of orange basket. Drizzle ½ teaspoon Grand Marnier in each basket.

3. Squeeze orange flesh to make ⅓ cup orange juice. Remove to a bowl. Add crabmeat and remaining ingredients; mix well. Spoon mixture into orange baskets. Place baskets in a heat-proof glass pie dish.

4. Prepare a wok for steaming (see page 29). Cover and steam orange baskets over high heat for 20 minutes.

Makes 4 servings

CHINESE "FIRSTS"

The bamboo steamer basket is just one of the many innovations that originated in China. Did you know that the Chinese can be credited with the invention of the clock? Not to mention the wok, the cleaver, the compass, printing, paper, porcelain (ever wonder why it's called China?) and gunpowder. Every time I return to China, I'm struck by the spirit of resourcefulness and improvisation that's an everyday way of life. People just seem to have a knack for making do and getting by. How else could a civilization continue to thrive for 5,000 years?

This is fried chicken Beijing-style, served with a spiced salt for dipping. Traditionally, chefs in Beijing start with a whole chicken, which is cut into eight pieces and deep-fried. Here's an easy, pan-fried adaptation. Cutting slashes parallel to the bone shortens the cooking time and allows the flavor of the marinade to permeate the meat.

EIGHT-PIECE BEIJING CHICKEN

FABULOUS FIVE-SPICE

The ancient Chinese believed the number five had curative powers, and the spice blend known as five-spice powder probably began as an herbal medicine. Like everything else nowadays, inflation has caught up with five-spice, and it usually has a few more than five ingredients, including star anise, cinnamon, fennel, clove, ginger, Sichuan peppercorn and dried tangerine peel, ground together into fine powder. It's delicious mixed with salt for dipping, and used on grilled or roasted foods.

8 chicken thighs or 8 drumsticks

Marinade
2 tablespoons rice wine
　　or dry sherry
2 tablespoons soy sauce
2 tablespoons cornstarch
2 tablespoons finely chopped green
　　onion
1 tablespoon grated ginger
2 teaspoons minced garlic

Spiced Salt
2 teaspoons salt
1 teaspoon Chinese five-spice
¼ teaspoon white pepper

3 tablespoons cooking oil

Method
1. If using chicken thighs, place chicken, skin side down, on a cutting board. With a sharp knife, cut slits ½-inch deep along both sides of the bone. Combine marinade ingredients in a bowl. Add chicken and stir to coat. Cover and refrigerate for 1 to 2 hours.

2. Combine spiced salt ingredients in a frying pan. Cook, stirring, over low heat, until toasted and fragrant, about 2 minutes. Let cool.

3. Place a wide frying pan over medium heat until hot. Add oil, swirling to coat sides. Add chicken and cook until golden brown on all sides, 2 to 3 minutes per side. Reduce heat to medium-low, cover, and cook until meat is no longer pink when cut, 10 to 12 minutes.

4. Serve chicken with spiced salt on the side.

Makes 4 servings

On the road to Xian, we spent the night at a farmhouse, the home of the Chan family. The next day, Mrs. Chan and her mother served us a wonderful outdoor lunch that included this spicy glazed chicken. When you're cooking whole chiles, stir-fry them very briefly—they burn easily.

GLAZED XIAN CHICKEN

¾ **pound boneless, skinless chicken**
2 **tablespoons oyster flavored sauce**

Sauce
⅓ **cup chicken broth**
3 **tablespoons rice wine**
   or dry sherry
2 **tablespoons regular soy sauce**
1 **tablespoon dark soy sauce**
1 **tablespoon rice vinegar**
1½ **tablespoons sugar**
1 **teaspoon chili garlic sauce**

2 **tablespoons cooking oil**
6 **small dried red chiles**
1 **tablespoon minced garlic**
2 **ribs celery, thinly sliced**
   diagonally
1 **small zucchini, thinly sliced**
   diagonally
1 **small onion, thinly sliced**
2 **teaspoons cornstarch dissolved**
   1 **tablespoon water (optional)**
⅓ **cup toasted walnut halves**

Method

1. Cut chicken into ¾-inch pieces. Place in a bowl and add oyster flavored sauce; stir to coat. Let stand for 10 minutes. Combine sauce ingredients in a bowl; set aside.

2. Place a wok over high heat until hot. Add oil, swirling to coat sides. Add chiles, and garlic; cook, stirring, until fragrant, about 10 seconds. Add chicken and stir-fry for 1 minute. Add celery, zucchini, and onion; stir-fry for 30 seconds. Add sauce and bring to a boil. Reduce heat to low, cover, and simmer for 3 minutes. If desired, add cornstarch solution and cook, stirring, until sauce boils and thickens. Add walnuts and toss to coat.

Makes 4 servings

DOWN ON THE FARM
The time we spent on the farm with the Chan family was an inspiration to all of us. With temperatures as low as -50°F and as high as 110°F, farm life is no picnic in this part of China. But people like the Chans seem to have a real sense of harmony with nature that keeps them going. It sounds trite, but it's really true: although these people are poor, their life is very rich. It's full of the joys and sorrows of the real world and deeply tied to the land—and to traditions that haven't changed for thousands of years.

This is my version of a favorite banquet dish that's often served on festive occasions as a symbol of longevity. The crisp, chilled lettuce makes a wonderful contrast to the warm filling, and the sweetness of the hoisin sauce marries all the flavors.

MINCED POULTRY WITH WALNUTS IN LETTUCE CUPS

ON ORDER

For a metropolis of 11 million people, Beijing has very little crime and violence. The traffic is mind-boggling, but there are surprisingly few accidents. Behind the apparent chaos, there's a deep sense of order. It stems, in part, from the teachings of the Chinese philosopher, Confucius, who believed that the way to preserve peace and social order was to adopt a moral code based on humanity towards others, respect for oneself and a sense of the dignity of human life. 2,500 years later his teaching is alive and well in China. You might say that beneath the *confusion*, the social structure remains *Confucian!*

½ pound boneless, skinless
    chicken, turkey, or duck
1 tablespoon oyster flavored sauce
6 dried black mushrooms
2 tablespoons cooking oil
1 teaspoon minced ginger
1 small carrot,
    cut into ¼-inch cubes
1 small zucchini,
    cut into ¼-inch cubes
1 cup diced water chestnuts
    or jicama
1 tablespoon rice wine
    or dry sherry
1 teaspoon sesame oil
¾ cup coarsely chopped
    toasted walnuts

12 small iceberg lettuce cups
Hoisin sauce

Method

1. Cut chicken into ¼-inch pieces. Place in a bowl and add oyster flavored sauce; stir to coat. Let stand for 10 minutes. Soak mushrooms in warm water to cover until softened, about 15 minutes; drain, reserving ¼ cup of the soaking liquid. Trim and discard stems. Chop caps.

2. Place a wok over high heat until hot. Add cooking oil, swirling to coat sides. Add ginger and cook, stirring, until fragrant, about 10 seconds. Add chicken and stir-fry for 1 minute. Add carrot, zucchini, and water chestnuts; stir-fry for 30 seconds.

3. Add reserved mushroom soaking liquid and cook until vegetables are crisp-tender, about 2 minutes. Add wine and sesame oil; cook until heated through. Add walnuts and toss to coat.

4. To eat, spread hoisin sauce on a lettuce cup, spoon in some of chicken mixture, wrap up in lettuce cup, and eat out of hand.

Makes 4 to 6 servings

Which came first, the chicken or the egg? In this case, it doesn't really matter! They're combined in a light, egg-whites-only scramble. For company, I serve it in crunchy lettuce cups. But for a simple family supper, I like to make it as an omelet by simply stir-frying the chicken, cooking the egg whites omelet-style and adding the chicken and ham as a filling.

CHICKEN AND EGG WHITE SCRAMBLE

LIGHT READING

If you're like most people nowadays, you're trying to eat lighter, healthier foods. Fortunately, the basic principles of Chinese cooking are already very healthful. Here are a few of my favorite ways to lighten up the foods you love:

• Substitute egg whites with a little milk for whole eggs.

• Try soy milk as a substitute for dairy products.

• Ask your butcher to help you choose leaner cuts of meat.

• Check out reduced-sodium soy sauce.

• Eat slowly, savor the moment, and have a little extra rice.

Marinade

1 tablespoon rice wine or dry sherry
2 teaspoons cornstarch
½ teaspoon sugar
½ teaspoon salt
⅛ teaspoon white pepper

½ pound boneless, skinless chicken, minced
6 egg whites, lightly beaten
2 tablespoons milk
½ teaspoon salt
2 tablespoons cooking oil
2 tablespoons chopped ham
4 small iceberg lettuce cups

Method

1. Combine marinade ingredients in a bowl. Add chicken and mix well. Let stand for 10 minutes.

2. Combine egg whites, milk, and salt in a bowl; set aside.

3. Place a non-stick frying pan over high heat until hot. Add 1 tablespoon oil, swirling to coat sides. Add chicken and stir-fry for 2 minutes. Remove the chicken from the pan.

4. Add remaining 1 tablespoon oil, swirling to coat sides. Add egg white mixture and cook, stirring, until eggs are softly set. Fold in chicken and ham. Spoon into lettuce cups and serve.

Makes 4 servings

*P*eking Duck is Beijing's most famous specialty—a banquet treat that's seldom prepared at home, since most Chinese kitchens don't have ovens. But since you probably do, here's how you can make your own tasty Peking Duck at home.

HOME-STYLE PEKING ROAST DUCK

1 duckling (4 to 5 pounds), cleaned

Marinade
2 tablespoons soy sauce
2 tablespoons hoisin sauce
3 slices ginger, lightly crushed

Glaze
1 ½ cups water
¼ cup rice vinegar
¼ cup honey or maltose
¼ teaspoon red food coloring
    (optional)

16 to 18 Mandarin Pancakes
    or flour tortillas
Hoisin sauce
Slivered green onions

Method
1. Parboil duck in a large pot of boiling water for 3 minutes; drain and pat dry with paper towels. Let cool slightly.

2. Combine marinade ingredients; rub inside duck cavity. Cover duck and refrigerate for 2 to 4 hours.

3. Combine glaze ingredients in a saucepan. Cook, stirring, over medium heat, until heated through. Turn off heat. Tie a string around duck's neck or under its wings.

Holding duck over the pan, ladle glaze over duck 6 to 8 times to coat all skin areas. Hang duck in a cool place until skin is taut and dry, 4 to 6 hours (2 hours if you use an electric fan).

4. Preheat oven to 400°F. Place duck, breast side up, on a rack in a foil-lined roasting pan. Roast, uncovered, for 40 minutes. Turn duck over; roast for 20 minutes, brushing occasionally with pan drippings. Turn duck breast side up again and brush with pan dripping. Roast until skin is brown and crisp, about 10 minutes.

5. Prepare a wok for steaming (see page 29). Wrap Mandarin Pancakes in a damp towel and place inside steamer. Cover and steam for about 3 minutes; keep warm.

6. Carve duck, including the crispy skin, into thin slices; arrange on a serving plate. To eat, spread hoisin sauce on a Mandarin Pancake, place 1 or 2 slices of duck on sauce, top with slivered green onions, roll up, and eat out of hand.

Makes 4 to 6 servings

DUCK TALES

Boy, were we served a lot of Peking Duck in Beijing. And we never got tired of it! The classic presentation begins with a series of appetizers made from the liver, gizzard, wings and feet, not to mention preserved duck eggs served with pickled ginger. Next comes the main event: platter after platter of thinly sliced duck—the crispy skin, and the succulent meat— along with pancakes or steamed buns, sweet hoisin sauce and green onions. Then there's the traditional soup, made from the duck carcass. And no duck banquet would be complete without the final touch: the *bill!*

75

A Mongolian hot pot is the Chinese version of fondue, and it's great for entertaining because it brings people together and, best of all, once you set it up, the guests do all the work! In the North, lamb is traditionally the main ingredient, while in the South it might be seafood, chicken or pork and lots of fresh vegetables. Finish off the meal by serving the flavorful broth as a soup.

MONGOLIAN HOT POT

ONE HOT POT!

When nomadic Mongol invaders under Genghis Kahn broke through the Great Wall and took Beijing in the 13th century, they brought with them a kind of portable stove: the Mongolian hot pot. When buying a hot pot, be sure to find one that's suitable for cooking—some are purely ornamental. Always fill the moat with hot broth *before* adding the coals to avoid damaging the pot. You can start the coals in a barbecue, then use tongs to transfer them to the hot pot, filling the chimney half-way full.

My ancient ancestor, Genghis Yan, takes a break from storming the Great Wall to enjoy a hot pot dinner.

6 cups chicken broth
2 slices ginger, lightly crushed
2 green onions, cut in half
    and lightly crushed
8 ounces dried bean thread noodles
2 pounds tender boneless lamb
    or beef
1 package (14 ounces) regular-firm
    tofu, drained
2 pounds leafy green vegetables,
such as bok choy, spinach,
    or napa cabbage

Dipping Sauce
½ cup soy sauce
3 tablespoons chicken broth
1 tablespoon sesame seed paste
    or chunky peanut butter
1 tablespoon sesame oil

Method
1. Place broth, ginger, and green onions in a large pot; bring to a boil. Reduce heat to low, cover, and simmer for 30 minutes. Discard ginger and green onions.

2. Soak bean thread noodles in warm water to cover until softened, about 15 minutes; drain. Cut bean thread noodles into 4-inch lengths. Cut lamb into thin slices. Cut tofu into 1-inch cubes. Cut vegetables into bite-size pieces. Arrange bean thread noodles, lamb, tofu, and vegetables on individual plates.

3. Combine dipping sauce ingredients in a bowl; whisk together until blended. Pour into individual dipping bowls.

4. Reheat broth to simmering. Set a Mongolian hot pot or an electric wok in center of table. Arrange individual plates and dipping bowls around hot pot. Pour broth into hot pot and adjust heat so broth simmers gently. Each diner cooks his or her choice of ingredients in the broth and seasons it with the dipping sauce.

Makes 6 to 8 servings

With its rich, savory sauce, fragrant with garlic and chiles, Mongolian beef is a favorite dish of the North—and a favorite Chinese restaurant dish throughout the world. For an authentic and dramatic presentation, serve it over snowy white crispy bean thread noodles (see column at right).

MONGOLIAN BEEF

Marinade
2 tablespoons dark soy sauce
2 tablespoons rice wine
    or dry sherry
1 teaspoon cornstarch

¾ pound flank steak, thinly sliced
2½ tablespoons cooking oil
2 tablespoons minced garlic
10 small dried red chiles
10 green onions,
    cut into 3-inch pieces
2 tablespoons hoisin sauce
1 tablespoon soy sauce

Method
1. Combine marinade ingredients in a bowl. Add beef and stir to coat. Let stand for 10 minutes.

2. Place a wok over high heat until hot. Add 2 tablespoons oil, swirling to coat sides. Add beef and stir-fry until barely pink, about 2 minutes. Remove the beef from the wok.

3. Add remaining ½ tablespoon oil to wok, swirling to coat sides. Add garlic, and chiles; cook, stirring, until fragrant, about 10 seconds.

4. Add green onions and stir-fry for 1 minute. Return beef to wok and add hoisin sauce and soy sauce. Cook until heated through.

Makes 4 servings

CRISPY BEAN THREADS

If you've never made crispy fried bean thread noodles, you're in for a surprise. On contact with the hot oil, the dried noodles puff up instantly creating a snowy white nest. Snip off a small amount of dried bean thread noodles using heavy-duty kitchen shears. Heat cooking oil for deep-frying to 375°F in a wok. Deep-fry bean threads in small batches until they puff and expand, about 5 seconds. Turn them over to cook the other side, then drain on paper towels.

Grilling is not a typical method of cooking in most parts of China, and grilled foods—like these small skewers of lamb—are most likely to be found at open-air food stands. When preparing them at home, pre-soak the bamboo skewers in water to help keep them from burning on the grill.

MONGOLIAN LAMB SKEWERS

¾ **pound tender boneless lamb**
    (or beef)

Marinade
⅓ **cup rice wine or dry sherry**
¼ **cup soy sauce**
2 **teaspoons minced garlic**
2 **teaspoons cornstarch**
1 **teaspoon ground toasted**
    Sichuan peppercorns

About 16 bamboo skewers
½ **tablespoon cooking oil**
1 **medium onion,**
    cut into ½-inch pieces

Method
1. Cut beef into thin strips, about ½-inch wide and 8-inches long. Combine marinade ingredients in a bowl. Add beef and stir to coat. Let stand for 10 minutes.

2. Soak skewers in warm water to cover for 15 minutes; drain.

3. Lift beef from marinade. Thread one piece of beef on each skewer, stretching beef so it lays flat. Reserve marinade.

4. To cook, place skewers on a greased grill 3 to 4 inches above a solid bed of glowing coals. Cook, basting with marinade, until beef is barely pink, about 1 minute on each side.

5. Place a wok over high heat until hot. Add oil, swirling to coat sides. Add onion and stir-fry until onion is crisp-tender, 3 to 4 minutes. Spread onion on a serving plate. Place skewered beef on top.

Makes 4 servings

XIAN STREET SCENE

Xian, the ancient capital of China, was once on a par with Rome and Constantinople for its size, splendor and cultural influence. It's home to one of the greatest archaeological discoveries in the world: the famous terracotta warriors, a 2,000-year-old army of more than 6,000 life-sized soldiers. Xian's outdoor night market is a great discovery, too. It's probably the world's largest open-air eating place, serving more than 20,000 people every night—a great place to try Moslem specialties, like grilled lamb.

This quick stir-fry of lamb with red, yellow and green onions and leeks was inspired by more than one restaurant dish we were served in Beijing. I love the way the sweetness of the onions and the tanginess of the vinegar bring out the flavor of the lamb.

WOK-SEARED LAMB WITH FOUR ONIONS

ON THE LAMB

Beijing is known as lamb capital of China. You can find lamb and mutton (which is lamb that's over a year old) on most restaurant menus, and in the streets you often smell the distinctive aroma of lamb cooking. In southern China, lamb is less readily available, and southerners, being unused to its strong flavor rarely serve it. I never even tasted lamb until I was 16 years old! To balance the pronounced taste of lamb, northern cooks prepare it with lots of onions, leeks and garlic, and season it with flavorful condiments like vinegar, chili sauce, rice wine and hoisin.

¾ pound boneless lamb
(leg or loin)

Marinade
2 tablespoons rice wine
or dry sherry
2 tablespoons dark soy sauce
2 teaspoons cornstarch
¼ teaspoon ground toasted Sichuan
peppercorns

Sauce
3 tablespoons hoisin sauce
1 tablespoon dark soy sauce
1 tablespoon vinegar
2 teaspoons chili garlic sauce

2½ tablespoons cooking oil
3 cloves garlic, thinly sliced
½ cup each thinly sliced red and
yellow onion
6 green onions, julienned
1 leek (white part only), julienned

Method
1. Cut lamb into thin slices then cut slices into thin strips. Combine marinade ingredients in a bowl. Add lamb and stir to coat. Let stand for 10 minutes. Combine sauce ingredients in a bowl; set aside.

2. Place a wok over high heat until hot. Add 2 tablespoons oil, swirling to coat sides. Add garlic and cook, stirring, until fragrant, about 10 seconds. Add lamb and stir-fry until barely pink, 1½ to 2 minutes. Remove the lamb from the wok.

3. Add remaining ½ tablespoon oil to wok, swirling to coat sides. Add red and yellow onions, green onions, and leek; stir-fry for 1 minute. Return lamb to wok and add sauce; cook until heated through.

Makes 4 servings

Here's a great way to roast a leg of lamb that's flavorful and easy to serve: start with a boneless leg, score the inside before marinating to allow the marinade to flavor the meat, then stuff the roast with green onions and roll it up. If you don't have time to make the Sesame Seed Pillows, you can serve the lamb with soft flour tortillas, or pita bread.

MONGOLIAN ROAST LAMB

1 boneless leg of lamb (3½ to 4
   pounds)

Marinade
6 slices ginger, lightly crushed
2 whole star anise
3 tablespoons coarsely
   chopped garlic
¼ cup rice wine or dry sherry
3 tablespoons char siu sauce
   or hoisin sauce
3 tablespoons soy sauce
1 tablespoon sesame oil
1 teaspoon ground toasted
   Sichuan peppercorns
1 teaspoon black pepper

4 to 6 green onions, trimmed
Sesame Seed Pillows
   (see page 42)

Method
1. Remove excess fat from lamb. Open boned leg and score inside. Combine marinade ingredients in a bowl. Rub marinade inside and outside of lamb. Cover and refrigerate for 4 to 6 hours.

2. Preheat oven to 325°F. Place green onions inside of meat. Reform lamb into a compact roll; tie tightly with kitchen string. Place lamb on a rack in a foil-lined roasting pan. Roast, uncovered, 25 to 30 minutes per pounds for rare (140°F) or 30 to 35 minutes per pound for medium (160°F).

3. Let rest for 15 minutes before carving. Serve with Sesame Seed Pillows.

Makes 6 to 8 servings

LEG OF LAMB

Boneless leg of lamb is a wonderful thing! Marinated and roasted and served as in this recipe, it gives you uniform, evenly cooked slices with an attractive filling at the center. It's also great for grilling. Just open it out, scoring the inside lightly so that it lies as flat as possible, and marinate or season it (Chinese five-spice, soy sauce, hosin and garlic are some of my favorite marinade ingredients). I like to start the meat on the barbecue, grilling both sides to brown and flavor it all over, then finish it in the oven so the inside is perfectly cooked.

Poached pears make a nice light dessert during the warmer months. If you can find Asian pears—also called "apple pears" because they look like a cross between a pear and an apple—give them a try. They have a pleasantly sweet flavor and a crunchy texture that stands up well to poaching. When the conversation lags, you can impress your guests with this piece of pear trivia: Asian pears are the oldest known cultivated pears in the world!

PEARS POACHED IN PLUM WINE

SWEET TALK

If you ever have the good fortune to be invited to a banquet in China and you're served a sweet dessert, don't get up and leave! The meal's not over! The northern and western Chinese sometimes serve sweets throughout the meal in the form of soups and fruit concoctions, and they don't build in a grand finale dessert as western cooks do. A meal is likely to end with slices of fresh fruit and a bowl of rice to aid in digestion. Fortune cookies, by the way, are a Chinese restaurant invention, originally from San Francisco, not China.

3 cups water
⅔ cup sugar
¼ cup plum wine
3 tablespoons lemon juice
4 slices ginger, lightly crushed
4 Asian pears or medium-firm
   ripe Bartlett or Bosc pears
2 tablespoons plum sauce
Chopped crystallized ginger
   for garnish

Method
1. Combine water, sugar, wine, lemon juice, and ginger in a saucepan. Bring to a boil over medium heat.

2. Peel pears with a vegetable peeler, keeping stems intact. If you wish, remove cores from bottom of pears with a melon baller.

3. As you peel each pear, place it in the liquid. Simmer, uncovered, until pears are barely tender, 20 to 30 minutes, depending on ripeness of fruit. Turn pears occasionally during cooking.

4. Lift out pears with a slotted spoon and place in a wide bowl. Simmer syrup until it is reduced to 1 cup. Add plum sauce to syrup; cook until heated through. Pour syrup over pears. Let stand until cool. Serve at room temperature or cover and refrigerate and serve cold. Sprinkle a little crystallized ginger over each serving for garnish.

Makes 4 servings

This Chinese-style nut brittle, seasoned with five-spice and sweetened with honey and brown sugar, is addictive. I like to serve it with hot tea. Keep a close eye on the nuts when you're deep-frying them. Once they begin to turn golden, they brown quickly, and if you don't watch out, you'll end up with Honey-Blazed Nut Snacks!

HONEY-GLAZED NUT SNACKS

Cooking oil for deep-frying
2 cups walnut halves
1 cup raw cashews
2 egg roll wrappers,
    cut into ½-inch squares

Glaze
¼ cup packed brown sugar
1 tablespoon butter
3 tablespoons honey
¼ teaspoon Chinese five-spice

2 teaspoons toasted sesame seeds

Method
1. Heat oil in a wok to 300°F over medium heat. Deep-fry walnuts and cashews and cook, turning frequently, until golden brown, 4 to 5 minutes. Remove and drain on paper towels.

2. Heat oil in a wok to 350°F over high heat. Deep-fry egg roll squares and cook, turning frequently, until golden brown, about 1 minute. Remove and drain on paper towels.

3. Combine brown sugar and butter in a saucepan. Cook, stirring, over low heat until brown sugar melts. Add honey and five-spice; mix well. Remove saucepan from heat and add nuts, egg roll squares, and sesame seeds; toss gently to coat.

4. Spread mixture in a foil-lined baking pan. Let stand until cool. Break into bite-size pieces before serving.

Makes 4 to 6 servings

SPEAKING "MANDARIN"
A final note before we leave the North. You sometimes hear about Mandarin cooking. Does this refer to northern or Beijing-style food? Yes and no. Mandarin, China's official language is the dialect spoken in Beijing. The word originally meant a high-ranking government official, and became attached to Beijing, the seat of the imperial court. But "Mandarin cuisine" is an American expression, originally used to distinguish Chinese restaurants that served foods other than Cantonese. Today, Americans tend to identify restaurants by regions, like Hunan, Sichuan and Shanghai, and the term Mandarin is used less and less.

These walnuts in Xian's open-air market come from the faraway and exotic USA!

Canton~Bounties

Guangzhou (Canton), the capital of the southern province, Guangdong, is a bustling port along the Pearl River. This lush region is known for its rich agriculture and its pure, fresh cooking.

Over the centuries, a great variety of natural products have been produced here, including ME! I was born in Guangzhou a short while ago! Guangzhou has more restaurants than any city in China because of the

of the Southland

abundance of fresh ingredients. Rice is plentiful here, along with a colorful array of vegetables and tropical fruits, from lychee and melon to citrus. Fresh- and salt-water fish, shell-fish, duck, squab, quail and chicken are widely used in dishes of spectacular simplicity—often steamed or stir-fried and served with light, clean sauces that show off the natural flavors and colors of the ingredients.

A "pei pa" is a Chinese lute, and that's just what these delicate butterflied shrimp look like. This dish is similar to the popular dim sum dish, shrimp toast, in which the shrimp filling is spread on a butterflied shrimp.

PEI PA SHRIMP

24 jumbo raw shrimp

Marinade
½ **egg white (1 tablespoon), lightly beaten**
2 **teaspoons rice wine or dry sherry**
½ **teaspoon sesame oil**
1 **tablespoon cornstarch**
½ **teaspoon salt**
¼ **teaspoon sugar**
¼ **teaspoon white pepper**

3 **tablespoons chopped water chestnuts**
Cornstarch for dry-coating
1 **ounce thinly sliced ham, julienned**
1 **sheet Japanese seaweed** (*nori*), **cut into thin strips**
3 **tablespoons cooking oil**
Prepared sweet and sour sauce

Method
1. Shell and devein 8 shrimp. Shell remaining 16 shrimp, leaving tails intact; butterfly them and rinse out sand veins. Combine marinade ingredients in a bowl. Add all shrimp and stir to coat. Let stand for 10 minutes.

2. Remove the 8 shelled and deveined shrimp. Place in a food processor and add water chestnuts; process to make a coarse paste.

3. To fill each shrimp, flatten the butterflied shrimp, then dredge, cut side down, in cornstarch. Shake to remove excess. Spread 1 tablespoon of shrimp mixture over cornstarch; smooth the mounded filling with a wet table knife. Center a strip of seaweed on filling; place a strip of ham on each side of seaweed.

4. Place a wok or wide frying pan over high heat until hot. Add oil, swirling to coat sides. Add shrimp, filling side down, and cook until prawns turn pink, 2 to 3 minutes.

5. Arrange shrimp on a serving plate and serve with sweet and sour sauce.

Makes 8 servings

Inspired by the sweet lotus and bean paste dumplings served in dim sum teahouses, these rice dumplings are easy to make, and they have a special twist: they're coated with vinagered rice in the manner of Japanese sushi.

RICE DUMPLINGS

⅔ cup rice vinegar
¼ cup sugar
1 ½ teaspoons salt
⅔ cup sweet lotus seed paste
⅔ cup sweet red bean paste
2 tablespoons toasted white
    sesame seeds
2 tablespoons black sesame seeds
5 cups hot cooked medium-grain
    rice
1 sheet Japanese seaweed *(nori),*
    cut into ¼-inch wide strips

Method
1. Combine vinegar, sugar, and salt in a saucepan. Cook, stirring, over medium heat until sugar dissolves; let cool.

2. Divide both lotus seed paste and red bean paste into 10 portions each. Roll each portion into a ball. Combine sesame seeds in a bowl; set aside.

3. Place hot rice into a shallow pan. Pour two-thirds vinegar mixture evenly over the surface. Fold in liquid; mix well.

4. Dip hands in remaining vinegar mixture to prevent rice from sticking to hands. To make each dumpling, spread ¼ cup warm rice in palm of hand. Place 1 ball of paste in center of rice; enclose filling with rice to cover and roll into a ball.

5. Dip lotus seed paste rice dumplings in sesame seed mixture and lightly press to secure coating. Wrap a strip of seaweed around red bean paste rice dumplings.

Makes 20

RICE IDEAS

When I was growing up in Guangzhou, rice was served at every meal—as a porridge (called *congee* or *jook*) for breakfast, and boiled, steamed or fried at lunch and dinner. Rice symbolizes nourishment and well-being in China. Spilling a bowl of rice is thought to bring bad luck, and serving poorly cooked rice to a guest is a great offense. When I was a kid, my mom used to tell me that for every grain of rice left behind in my bowl a freckle would appear on the face of my future wife. It worked! My wife doesn't have freckles and I still never waste a grain of rice!

A light soup that's typically Cantonese: the simple broth allows the delicately sweet flavor of the fresh crabmeat to come through. If you think of watercress as having a bitter flavor, you're probably used to eating it stem and all. Take an extra minute or two to pick through it, leaving only the leaves and the most tender stems, and you'll be surprised at the mildness of its flavor.

WATERCRESS SOUP WITH CRAB

Marinade
2 teaspoons cornstarch
½ teaspoon salt

¼ pound cooked crabmeat, flaked
2 teaspoons cooking oil
3 slices ginger, lightly crushed
4 cups chicken broth
1 cup water
1 bunch watercress (about ¾ pound),
   tough stems removed
½ cup sliced carrots
½ teaspoon sesame oil
¼ teaspoon white pepper

Method
1. Combine marinade ingredients in a bowl. Add crabmeat and stir to coat. Let stand for 10 minutes.

2. Place a 2-quart pot over high heat until hot. Add cooking oil, swirling to coat sides. Add ginger and cook, stirring, until fragrant, about 10 seconds. Add crabmeat and stir-fry for 1 minute.

3. Add broth and water; bring to a boil. Add watercress and carrots. Reduce heat to low and simmer until vegetables are tender, about 5 minutes. Stir in sesame oil and pepper.

Makes 4 to 6 servings

SOUP'S ON

In Chinese restaurants everywhere, the menu begins with appetizers and soups. Everywhere but in China, that is. Whether served at home or as part of a restaurant banquet, soup is seldom a course of its own in China. It's intended more as a beverage, to accompany the meal and wash down the mouthfuls of rice, meat and vegetables. At a banquet, a richer soup might be served with a light vegetable dish, and a vegetable soup with a meat dish. Hot sweet soups might be served toward the end of the meal.

The earthy flavor of shiitake mushrooms enhances this simple, clear soup that's as comforting as it is quick to prepare. Pour the mushroom soaking liquid through a coffee filter or fine mesh strainer and save it to use as a base for sauces, soups and stews.

MUSHROOMS IN FRAGRANT BROTH

MUSHROOMS, CUT & DRIED

When you are served black mushrooms at a Chinese restaurant, you're actually eating reconstituted dried mushrooms, not fresh ones. Like sun-dried tomatoes or raisins, dried black mushrooms have a much more intense, concentrated flavor than their fresh counterparts—a flavor the Chinese prefer. Dried black mushrooms, also known by their Japanese name, *shiitake,* are one of my favorite "chef's secrets." They keep almost indefinitely, they're easy to rehydrate (see page 37) and they give foods a rich, meaty flavor—the essence of mushroominess!

8 dried black mushrooms
¼ cup dried cloud ears (optional)

<u>Broth</u>
4 cups chicken broth
2 tablespoons soy sauce
½ teaspoon sesame oil
¼ teaspoon white pepper

½ pound boneless, skinless chicken breast halves
4 white button mushrooms, sliced
2 baby bok choy, quartered lengthwise

<u>Method</u>
1. Soak black mushrooms and cloud ears in warm water to cover until softened, about 15 minutes; drain. Trim and discard stems. Leave mushroom caps whole and thinly slice cloud ears. Cut chicken into thin slices then cut slices into thin strips.

2. Combine fragrant broth ingredients in a 2-quart pot; bring to a boil. Add black mushrooms and cloud ears. Reduce heat to low and simmer for 5 minutes.

3. Add button mushrooms and bok choy; simmer for 3 minutes. Add chicken and simmer until it is no longer pink, 2 to 3 minutes.

Makes 4 servings

Fruit-based sauces and dressings are relatively new innovations being introduced by creative young Chinese chefs, and this sweet and savory shrimp salad is a delicious example. Instead of grilling, you can also broil, poach, steam or pan-fry the shrimp.

SHRIMP SALAD WITH TROPICAL FRUIT SALSA

Marinade
1 tablespoon rice wine or dry sherry
1 teaspoon sesame oil
¼ teaspoon salt
¼ teaspoon white pepper

¾ pound medium raw shrimp,
    shelled and deveined

Dressing
3 tablespoons lime juice
    or rice vinegar
2 tablespoons plum sauce
2 tablespoons cooking oil
1½ tablespoons honey
1 tablespoon sesame oil
¼ teaspoon white pepper

Salsa
1 mango or papaya
¼ cup golden raisins
¼ cup diced red bell pepper
1 tablespoon chopped cilantro
1 tablespoon chopped crystallized
    ginger
3 tablespoons rice vinegar
1 teaspoon chili garlic sauce

4 cups mixed salad greens

Method
1. Combine marinade ingredients in a bowl. Add shrimp and stir to coat. Let stand for 10 minutes. Place shrimp on a greased grill 3 to 4 inches above a solid bed of glowing coals. Cook until shrimp turn pink, 1½ to 2 minutes on each side. Remove to a bowl and let cool. Cover and refrigerate until chilled.

2. Combine dressing ingredients in a bowl; set aside.

3. Prepare salsa: Peel mango. Cut one-half of the flesh into 4 slices and reserve for garnish. Cut the remaining fruit into ¼-inch cubes and place in a bowl with remaining salsa ingredients.

4. Place salad greens in a large bowl; add dressing and toss to coat. Divide greens among 4 salad plates. Arrange shrimp on one side of greens; spoon salsa on greens opposite the shrimp. Garnish each salad with a slice of mango.

Makes 4 servings

PLUM TASTY

Plum sauce is one of those ingredients I always keep on hand and use to give dishes a touch of sweet-tart flavor. It's a chunky, light amber, jam-like sauce, made from salted plums, apricots, yams, rice vinegar, chiles, sugar and spices. The fruity flavor of plum sauce goes well with roasted meats and poultry, and you'll often find it used as a dipping sauce with duck or goose in Canton. In the eastern U.S., it's sometimes used as the base for a restaurant concoction called "duck sauce" that's served with roasted or Peking duck.

When tofu is pan-fried until golden, its surface becomes slightly spongy, and it absorbs sauces well. Here, it's paired with three kinds of mushrooms, first stir-fried, then braised in a rich brown sauce.

BRAISED TOFU AND MUSHROOMS

TOUGHER TOFU

Soft or "silky" tofu has a custardy texture, and it's best for soups or making dressings. Firm tofu, which comes in more solid blocks, is best for stir-frying and deep-frying. If your tofu is a bit too soft, you can easily make it firmer. Cut the block of tofu in half lengthwise and lay the two halves on a flat surface lined with towels. Top with a flat weight, such as a platter, and let sit for half an hour. Some of the liquid will be extracted, and the tofu will become more solid. Parboiling tofu briefly in water before using it will also help to firm it up.

1 package (14 ounces) extra-firm
    tofu, drained

Sauce
⅔ cup vegetable broth
2 teaspoons black bean garlic sauce
2 teaspoons oyster flavored sauce
½ teaspoon sesame oil
1 teaspoon sugar

2 tablespoons cooking oil
½ pound small white button
    mushrooms
¼ pound oyster mushrooms
6 medium fresh shiitake mushrooms
1½ teaspoons cornstarch
    dissolved in 1 tablespoon water

Method
1. Cut tofu in half horizontally to make 2 pieces, each about ¾-inch thick. With a 2-inch biscuit cutter, cut 6 rounds from each half to make a total of 12 rounds. Combine sauce ingredients in a bowl; set aside.

2. Place a wide frying pan over medium-high heat until hot. Add 1 tablespoon oil, swirling to coat sides. Add tofu and cook until golden brown, 1½ to 2 minutes on each side. Remove the tofu from the wok.

3. Place a wok over high heat until hot. Add remaining 1 tablespoon oil, swirling to coat sides. Add all mushrooms and stir-fry for 1 minute. Add sauce, reduce heat to low, cover, and simmer until mushrooms are tender, about 5 minutes. Add cornstarch solution and cook, stirring, until sauce boils and thickens.

4. To serve, arrange tofu in a circle around edge of a serving plate. Place mushrooms in the center.

Makes 4 to 6 servings

I like to contrast the crunchy texture of fresh vegetables like sugar snap peas or snow peas with chewy pressed bean curd. Sold in Asian markets, it's bean curd that has been pressed with weights to extract some of its liquid until it's very firm and compact. You can find it plain or marinated with seasonings like soy sauce, star anise and five-spice.

PEA PODS WITH PRESSED BEAN CURD

OYSTER SAUCE

Where would we be without oyster sauce? Probably not in Southern China, where it's one of the basic building blocks of restaurant and home cooking. Oyster sauce is made from oyster extract, sugar, salt and seasonings, but don't be put off by fears of fishy flavor. Once cooked, it is sweet, slightly smoky, and wonderfully savory, enhancing the flavors of meat, poultry and seafood, and adding richness to vegetarian dishes. Speaking of which, you can even buy vegetarian oyster-flavored sauce which gets much of its flavor from black mushrooms.

Sauce
¼ cup chicken broth
2 tablespoons rice wine
    or dry sherry
2 tablespoons soy sauce
1 tablespoon oyster flavored sauce
1 teaspoon cornstarch

2 teaspoons cooking oil
¼ pound sugar snap peas
    or snow peas, trimmed
6 white button mushrooms, sliced
1 small zucchini, sliced
¼ cup sliced water chestnuts
¼ cup chicken broth
8 ounces spicy pressed bean curd,
    cut into ½-inch cubes

Method
1. Combine sauce ingredients in a bowl; set aside.

2. Place a wok over high heat until hot. Add oil, swirling to coast sides. Add sugar snap peas, mushrooms, zucchini, and water chestnuts; stir-fry for 1 minute. Add broth, cover, and cook until vegetables are crisp-tender, about 3 minutes. Add pressed bean curd and sauce; cook, stirring, until sauce boils and thickens.

Makes 4 servings

As a southerner, I grew up eating—and loving—simple foods, like steamed vegetables and savory egg custards, drizzled with a little oyster sauce. Here's a typical Cantonese-style recipe that's light and healthful, and works well with almost any kind of steamed seasonal vegetables.

STEAMED GARDEN VEGETABLES

3 Shanghai baby bok choy, cut in half lengthwise
1 cup broccoli florets
1 cup cauliflower florets

Sauce
½ cup chicken broth
2 tablespoons oyster flavored sauce
1 tablespoon rice wine or dry sherry
⅛ teaspoon white pepper

2 teaspoons cornstarch dissolved in 1 tablespoon water

Method
1. Prepare a wok for steaming (see page 29). Cover and steam vegetables over high heat until they are crisp-tender, 5 to 6 minutes.

2. Combine sauce ingredients in a saucepan; bring to a boil. Add cornstarch solution and cook, stirring, until sauce boils and thickens.

3. To serve, arrange vegetables on a serving plate and pour sauce over the top.

Makes 4 servings

VEGETABLE MATTERS

Nowadays, the produce section of my local supermarket is starting to look more and more like a Chinese grocery with new Asian vegetables appearing every week. Naturally, I'm delighted! Give these "new" vegetables a try. Chinese Broccoli *(Gai Lan)* is leafier than western broccoli and has delicate white flowers and a mild bitter-sweet flavor. If you like bok choy, try baby bok choy, or pale green Shanghai bok choy, which are sweeter and more tender than regular bok choy.

Tomato-based sweet and sour sauces were introduced to the West by way of southern China. This banquet-style dish is a nice way to add a lot of flavor to mild, white fish, and the presentation is elegant and attractive. To save time, you can use a prepared Asian-style sweet and sour sauce.

SWEET AND SOUR FISH ROLLS

BANQUET BASICS

You say you've been invited to a Chinese banquet? Here are some pointers. For birthdays and weddings, people wear red, but for funerals, they wear black or white. You'll probably be seated at a table for 10, with the place of honor furthest from the entrance (it's impolite to change seats). Serve yourself from the revolving tray in the center of the table once the guests of honor have been served. It's OK to use your hands (not chopsticks) to eat food that has bones or shells. The #1 rule: Smile and enjoy yourself. Remember, life is a banquet!

4 dried black mushrooms
1 pound firm white fish fillets, such as sea bass or red snapper, each about ½-inch thick
½ teaspoon salt
¼ teaspoon white pepper
1 small carrot, julienned
1 rib celery, julienned
2 green onions, julienned

Sauce
⅓ cup orange juice
¼ cup water
¼ cup ketchup
1 tablespoon lemon juice
½ teaspoon chili sauce
3 tablespoons sugar
1 tablespoon cornstarch
1 teaspoon minced ginger
½ teaspoon salt

Method
1. Soak mushrooms in warm water to cover until softened, about 15 minutes; drain. Trim and discard stems. Thinly slice caps.

2. Cut fish crosswise to make 2-inch by 3-inch pieces. Parallel cut each piece as illustrated so each piece is about ¼-inch thick. Sprinkle salt and pepper over fish. To make each roll, place 1 or 2 pieces of mushroom, carrot, celery, and green onion on short side of fish then roll fish into a cylinder.

3. Place fish rolls, seam side down, without crowding, in a heat-proof glass pie dish. Prepare a wok for steaming (see page 29). Cover and steam fish rolls over high heat until fish turns opaque, 5 to 6 minutes.

4. Combine sauce ingredients and 3 tablespoons steaming juices in a saucepan. Heat sauce over medium heat and cook, stirring, until sauce boils and thickens.

5. Arrange fish rolls on a serving plate and pour sauce over the top.

Makes 4 servings

Tomatoes are a popular ingredient in Cantonese sauces, and the combination of a fragrant, spicy tomato sauce and the mildness of soft bean curd is a winner. Use soft tofu for this dish, and don't be alarmed if it breaks down. That's the idea: a silky, smooth texture and a bold, assertive sauce—yin and yang in harmony.

BEAN CURD WITH SWEET TOMATO SAUCE

BEAN CURD WORDS

The soybean has been called "the cow of China," because it's a source of so many high-protein, low-fat products, many of which take the place of what westerners would call dairy products. Bean curd (known in China as *doufu* and in Japan as *tofu*, the name most often used in the U.S.) is made in much the same way as cheese, by extracting soy milk from cooked soybeans, curdling it, draining the curds and pressing them together into blocks. The more whey is pressed out, the firmer the bean curd becomes.

1 package (16 ounces) soft tofu
    (bean curd), drained
1 small onion
2 small tomatoes

Sauce
¼ cup ketchup
2 tablespoons hoisin sauce
1 tablespoon soy sauce
1 teaspoon chili garlic sauce

1 tablespoon cooking oil
2 teaspoons minced ginger
6 whole fresh basil leaves

Method
1. Cut tofu and onion into ½-inch cubes. Peel tomatoes and cut into ½-inch cubes. Combine sauce ingredients in a bowl; set aside.

2. Place a wok over high heat until hot. Add oil, swirling to coat sides. Add onion, and ginger; stir-fry for 1 minute. Add tofu and cook for 1 minute. Add tomatoes and basil; cook for 1 minute. Add sauce and cook until heated through.

Makes 4 servings

You'll find vegetable and tofu dishes like this one, sometimes called "Buddhist's Delight," all over southern China, where fresh produce is plentiful. Served over rice, it makes a complete, healthful meal that will delight you, even if you're not a vegetarian!

VEGETARIAN DELIGHT

8 dried black mushrooms
½ package (7 ounces) regular-firm
tofu, drained

Sauce
¾ cup vegetable broth
2 tablespoons soy sauce
2 teaspoons sesame oil
1½ teaspoons sugar
¼ teaspoon white pepper

1 tablespoon cooking oil
1 teaspoon minced ginger
1 small carrot, sliced
½ cup sliced bamboo shoots
1 can (15 ounces) baby corn,
drained
½ pound napa cabbage,
cut into 1-inch by 2-inch pieces
2 teaspoons cornstarch dissolved
in 1 tablespoon water

Method

1. Soak mushrooms in warm water to cover until softened, about 15 minutes; drain. Trim and discard stems. Quarter caps. Cut tofu into ½-inch cubes. Combine sauce ingredients in bowl; set aside.

2. Place a wok over high heat until hot. Add oil, swirling to coat sides. Add ginger and cook, stirring, until fragrant, about 10 seconds. Add mushrooms, carrot, bamboo shoots, baby corn, and cabbage; stir-fry for 1 minute. Add tofu and sauce; bring to a boil. Reduce heat to low, cover, and simmer until vegetables are tender, 4 to 5 minutes. Add cornstarch solution and cook, stirring, until sauce boils and thickens.

Makes 4 to 6 servings

MEATLESS MIRACLES

Vegetarian cooking was introduced to China in the kitchens of Buddhist and Taoist monasteries more than 2,000 years ago. The practice of abstaining from eating meat was originally tied to a belief in reincarnation. Over the centuries, Chinese vegetarian cooking has developed into a sophisticated cuisine in its own right. Cooks use a variety of protein-rich foods to simulate the flavors and textures of meat. Bean curd skin, for example, becomes mock poultry and wheat gluten stands in for meat. I often like the understudy better than the real thing!

Helping prepare lunch for 200 at the Shaolin Monastery.

My favorite way to eat deep-fried fish is with a spicy sweet and sour sauce. The traditional method of scoring the fillets before frying exposes more surface area, allowing the light, seasoned egg coating to cover more of the fish. As the fish fries, the score marks open up, and the result is dramatic and attractive.

PORCUPINE FISH WITH SWEET CHILI SAUCE

CORNSTARCH COMMENTS

Starches of all kinds are an essential part of Chinese cooking, but in the western world, the kind most widely used in Chinese food is cornstarch. This dish is a good illustration of what it can do. Dissolved in water, it's used to thicken sauces, giving them an attractive transparent glaze. As a coating, it seals in the juices of deep-fried foods and gives them a crispy exterior. In marinades, it helps coat foods evenly and gives them a velvety texture. I guess you could call it a *cornerstone* of Chinese cooking!

Sauce
¼ cup chicken broth
¼ cup rice vinegar
3 tablespoons ketchup
2 tablespoons sugar
1 tablespoon soy sauce
1 teaspoon chili sauce
2 teaspoons cornstarch

1 large firm white fish fillet
    (about 1 pound) with skin intact,
    such as sea bass or red snapper,
    about 1-inch thick
½ cup all-purpose flour
¼ cup cornstarch
¾ teaspoon salt
¼ teaspoon white pepper
Cooking oil for deep-frying
2 eggs, lightly beaten

Method
1. Combine sauce ingredients in a saucepan; set aside.

2. Score skinless side of fish with shallow diagonal cuts; score again at a 90° angle to the first cuts. Combine flour, cornstarch, salt, and pepper on a plate.

3. Heat oil in a wok to 375°F. Dip fish in egg, drain briefly, then dredge in flour mixture. Shake to remove excess. Deep-fry fish, and cook, turning once, until golden brown, 2 to 3 minutes. Remove and drain on paper towels.

4. Heat sauce over medium heat and cook, stirring, until sauce boils and thickens. To serve, arrange fish on a plate and pour sauce over the top.

Makes 4 servings

The traditional Chinese method of steaming fish is more than just healthful. By cutting slits in the fish and inserting complementary ingredients, you infuse it with flavor. This recipe works well with any firm-fleshed white fish, and smoked ham can be used instead of bacon.

STEAMED FISH WITH FIERY BLACK BEAN SAUCE

6 dried black mushrooms
3 slices lean smoked bacon
1½ pounds salmon fillets with
    skin, each about 1-inch thick
1 tablespoon cornstarch
¼ teaspoon white pepper
¼ cup sliced green onions

Sauce
1 tablespoon minced shallot
1 teaspoon minced jalapeno
    or serrano chile
3 tablespoons rice wine
    or dry sherry
2 tablespoons black bean garlic
    sauce
2 teaspoons sesame oil
2 teaspoons cooking oil
1 teaspoon sugar

Method

1. Soak mushrooms in warm water to cover until softened, about 15 minutes; drain. Trim and discard stems. Halve caps. Cut bacon into 3-inch pieces.

2. Cut fish crosswise into 4 large pieces. Cut 3 lengthwise slits, ¾-inch deep on skinless side of each fish piece. Sprinkle cornstarch and pepper over fish. Let stand for 10 minutes. Place a mushroom half, a few green onion slices, and a bacon piece in each slit.

3. Place fish in a heat-proof glass pie dish. Combine sauce ingredients in a bowl; pour over fish. Prepare a wok for steaming (see page 29). Cover and steam fish over high heat until fish turns opaque, 6 to 8 minutes.

Makes 4 servings

FRESH FISH FACTS

Living in coastal California, I'm spoiled by all the wonderful fresh seafood. But fish sometimes sits too long in the market, and it gets more spoiled than me! When buying a whole fish, judge it first by your eyes...and the fish's, which should be clear, not cloudy. Check the gills, which should be bright red. Then use your nose to detect any off or fishy odors. Finally use your ears: get the salesperson to tell you what's fresh that day. For fillets and steaks avoid those that are sitting in a pool of liquid. Chances are, they've gone the way of all fish.

Making bamboo steamers by hand.

Perhaps you've tried fish baked in a parchment wrapper. Why not serve it the Asian way, wrapped and steamed in a leafy packet? It's fun to open at the table, and the leaves impart a subtle flavor and perfume to the fish. Dried bamboo leaves can be found in many Asian markets.

FISH IN A BAMBOO LEAF

A NEW LEAF

Leave it to the Chinese to come up with all kinds of wonderful ways to cook food in leaves! Lotus leaves, which are sold dried and must be soaked before using, are large and round (almost 2 feet in di- ameter) with a pointed peak in the center that's perfect for stuffing. They give food an exotic, sweet, tea-like flavor. I love the classic dish, *Nor Mai Gai:* sticky rice cooked with chicken, ham or Chinese sausage, wrapped in a lotus leaf and steamed. Bamboo leaves, also used for wrap- ping and steaming food, are, like lotus leaves, inedible (un- less you're a panda bear).

1 ½ **pounds firm white fish fillets, such as sea bass or red snapper, each about ¾-inch thick**
2 **dried bamboo leaves or fresh** *ti* **leaves**

Sauce
2 **teaspoons chopped ginger**
2 **tablespoons black bean garlic sauce**
2 **tablespoons chicken broth**
2 **tablespoons dark soy sauce**
2 **teaspoons chili garlic sauce**
2 **teaspoons sesame oil**
1 **tablespoon sugar**
2 **teaspoons cornstarch**

3 **green onions, julienned**
2 **ounces thinly sliced ham, julienned**

Method

1. Cut fish crosswise to make 2-inch by 3-inch pieces. Soak leaves in warm water to cover for 30 minutes; drain. Cut leaves crosswise into 5-inch pieces.

2. Combine sauce ingredients in a bowl; set aside.

3. Place leaves, ribbed side up, on work surface. Center a piece of fish on each leaf piece. Top each piece with a heaping tablespoon of sauce and a few pieces of green onion and ham.

4. Fold sides of leaf around fish to enclose; secure with a wooden pick. Ends of packets will be open. Place fish packets in a heat-proof glass pie dish.

5. Prepare a wok for steaming (see page 29). Cover and steam fish packets over high heat until fish turns opaque, 6 to 8 minutes.

Makes 4 servings

This is my version of the famous southern specialty, Hakka Bean Curd. Triangles of tofu are stuffed with minced seafood, browned in a wok, and braised with vegetables in a seasoned broth.

HOME-STYLE BEAN CURD WITH SEAFOOD MOUSSE

STUFFING BEAN CURD

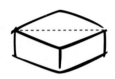

Cut tofu squares diagonally.

Scoop out tofu from long side.

Stuff with filling.

6 ounces firm white fish fillets or medium raw shrimp, shelled and deveined

Marinade
1 teaspoon chopped cilantro
1 tablespoon rice wine or dry sherry
1 tablespoon soy sauce
¼ egg white (1 tablespoon), lightly beaten
2 teaspoons cornstarch
¼ teaspoon salt

1 package (14 ounces) regular-firm tofu (bean curd), drained
2 tablespoons cooking oil

Broth
2½ cups chicken broth
2 tablespoons oyster flavored sauce
2 tablespoons soy sauce
1 teaspoon sesame oil
⅛ teaspoon white pepper

½ cup sliced bamboo shoots
½ cup sliced carrots
½ cup sliced zucchini

Method
1. Finely mince fish. Combine marinade ingredients in a bowl. Add fish and mix well. Let stand for 10 minutes.

2. Cut tofu in half horizontally to make 2 pieces, each about ¾-inch thick. Cut each half diagonally to form 4 triangles as illustrated. Using a melon baller or teaspoon, remove about 1 tablespoon tofu from longest side of each triangle.

3. Stuff each triangle with a heaping tablespoon of seafood mixture; smooth the mounded filling with the back of a wet spoon.

4. Place a wok over medium heat until hot. Add oil, swirling to coat sides. Add tofu triangles, filling side down, and cook until golden brown, 1 to 2 minutes. Place tofu triangles in a clay pot or a 2-quart pot.

5. Add seasoned broth ingredients and bring to a boil over medium heat. Reduce heat to low, cover, and simmer for 8 minutes. Add bamboo shoots, carrots, and zucchini. Cover and simmer until vegetables are crisp-tender, 3 to 4 minutes.

Makes 4 to 6 servings

Sweet, tender lychees are stuffed with a filling of minced prawns, coated in a light tempura-like batter and deep-fried until golden brown. If you have a pastry bag, you can use it to pipe the filling into the lychees.

PRAWN-STUFFED LYCHEES

Batter
⅔ cup all-purpose flour
¼ cup cornstarch
1¼ teaspoons baking powder
¾ cup ice water
1 tablespoon cooking oil

6 ounces medium raw prawns,
    shelled and deveined
½ egg white (1 tablespoon),
    lightly beaten
½ teaspoon salt
⅛ teaspoon white pepper
1 tablespoon finely chopped water
    chestnuts

Sauce
⅓ cup prepared sweet and sour
    sauce
1 teaspoon grated lemon peel

1 can (15 ounces) lychees, drained
Cornstarch for dry-coating
Cooking oil for deep-frying
Cantaloupe balls for garnish

Method
1. Prepare batter: Combine flour, cornstarch, and baking powder in a bowl. Add ice water and oil. Mix batter until smooth. Cover and refrigerate for 1 hour.

2. Finely chop prawns. Place in a bowl and add egg white, salt, and pepper; stir to coat. Let stand for 10 minutes. Add water chestnuts and mix well. Combine sauce ingredients in a bowl; set aside.

3. Dry lychees with paper towels. Fill each lychee with a rounded teaspoon of prawn mixture. Roll stuffed lychees in cornstarch.

4. Heat oil in a wok to 330°F. Dip several stuffed lychees into batter; drain briefly. Deep-fry stuffed lychees and cook, turning occasionally, until golden brown, about 5 minutes. Remove and drain on paper towels.

5. Arrange stuffed lychees on a serving plate and garnish with cantaloupe balls. Serve sauce on the side.

Makes 4 servings

SHRIMP OR PRAWNS?

People always ask me "what's the difference between prawns and shrimp?" The answer is that there's no single answer. Some people will tell you that prawns are larger, but others say jumbo shrimp and prawns are the same thing. Some claim prawns are freshwater dwellers and shrimp live in salt water. Personally, I think it all depends what part of the English speaking world you live in. Whatever the locals call them, I always call them one thing: delicious!

Even if you don't have a sizzle platter to serve this on, it's got plenty of sizzle of its own from fresh chiles, garlic, ginger and onion.

SIZZLING OYSTERS AND MUSSELS

¾ pound mussels, cleaned

Marinade
2 teaspoons cornstarch
½ teaspoon salt

1 jar (10 to 12 ounces) shucked
    oysters, drained

Sauce
¼ cup chicken broth
3 tablespoons rice wine
    or dry sherry
1 tablespoon black bean garlic sauce
1 tablespoon dark soy sauce
1 teaspoon cornstarch
½ teaspoon sugar

2 tablespoons cooking oil
1 jalapeño or serrano chili, minced
1 green onion, thinly sliced
3 cloves garlic, sliced
4 slices ginger, lightly crushed
2 teaspoons cornstarch dissolved in
    1 tablespoon water
½ teaspoon sesame oil

Method

1. Place mussels in a heat-proof glass pie dish. Prepare a wok for steaming (see page 29). Cover and steam mussels over high heat until shells open, 3 to 4 minutes. Let cool. Strain and reserve ½ cup of mussel steaming liquid; discard sandy residue.

2. Combine marinade ingredients in a bowl. Add oysters and stir to coat. Let stand for 10 minutes. Parboil oysters in a pot of boiling water for 1 minute; drain.

3. Combine sauce ingredients in a bowl; set aside.

4. Place a wok over high heat until hot. Add cooking oil, swirling to coat sides. Add chili, green onion, garlic, and ginger; cook, stirring, until fragrant, about 10 seconds. Add steamed mussels, reserved mussel steaming liquid, oysters, and sauce; bring to a boil. Add cornstarch solution and cook, stirring, until sauce boils and thickens. Stir in sesame oil.

5. Place on a serving plate. If you wish to make dish sizzle, serve on a pre-heated cast-iron serving plate.

Makes 4 servings

MUSSEL FITNESS

How can you spot a fresh mussel? It should be alive, and that means it should either be closed tightly or should close quickly when you pick it up. In the store, make sure the two halves of the shell don't slide back and forth easily. If they do, you're probably holding a mussel full of mud. Quick! Put it back! Once cooked, the muscle in the mussel no longer clamps the shell tightly, and it opens. If a cooked mussel doesn't open, don't eat it.

Fruit and duck are a natural combination in the cuisines of many cultures. They go together splendidly in this quick, Southern-style stir-fry of tender duck breast with a sweet, fruity sauce and chunks of lychee and pineapple. Boneless duck breast is sold fresh, and sometimes frozen in many major supermarkets. A boneless half breast tends to weigh in at around 8 ounces.

LYCHEE-PINEAPPLE DUCK

I LOVE LYCHEE

Southern China is the land of lychees. But nowadays, so is the American South. Florida growers produce fresh lychees from July through September—which is great news for me, because ever since I was a small boy, I've never been able to get enough of them. If you ever get a chance to taste fresh lychees you'll understand why. Fortunately, canned lychees are always available, and I love their sweet flavor and soft texture, too. In Canton, you'll find ly-chees used in sweet and sour dishes and sometimes served as a refreshment over a bowl of ice.

½ **pound boneless, skinless duck breast**

Marinade
1 tablespoon rice wine or dry sherry
2 teaspoons dark soy sauce
2 teaspoons cornstarch

Sauce
3 tablespoons plum sauce
3 tablespoons pineapple juice
2 tablespoons chicken broth
1 tablespoon soy sauce
½ teaspoon cornstarch

1 ½ tablespoons cooking oil
2 slices ginger, lightly crushed
1 red bell pepper, cut into 1-inch squares
½ cup lychees
½ cup pineapple chunks

Method
1. Cut duck breast into thin slices. Combine marinade ingredients in a bowl. Add duck and stir to coat. Let stand for 10 minutes. Combine sauce ingredients in a bowl; set aside.

2. Place a wok over high heat until hot. Add oil, swirling to coat sides. Add ginger and cook, stirring, until fragrant, about 10 seconds Add duck and stir-fry until duck is cooked through but still rosy, 1 to 2 minutes. Remove the duck from the wok.

3. Add bell pepper, lychees, and pineapple to wok; stir-fry for 1 minute. Return duck to wok and add sauce; cook, stirring, until sauce boils and thickens.

Makes 4 servings

The term "white-cut" refers to the process of cooking foods—especially chicken—without soy sauce, by first slowly simmering and then steeping in cold water several times during poaching. This method produces extraordinarily juicy, delicate chicken, and, though it's found all over China, I think of it as typical of the Cantonese passion for clean, fresh flavors. White-cut chicken is best when served with a simple toasted Sichuan pepper salt or a little oyster sauce on the side for dipping.

WHITE-CUT CHICKEN WITH PEPPER SALT

Marinade
¼ cup rice wine or dry sherry
1 ½ teaspoons salt
¼ teaspoon white pepper

1 whole frying chicken (3 to 3 ½ pounds), cleaned
3 green onions, cut in half and lightly crushed
6 slices ginger, lightly crushed
1 whole star anise

Pepper Salt
2 teaspoons salt
1 teaspoon ground toasted Sichuan peppercorns
¼ teaspoon Chinese five-spice
¼ teaspoon white pepper

Method
1. Combine marinade ingredients in a bowl. Rub marinade inside and outside of chicken. Cover and refrigerate for 2 hours.

2. Bring a pot of water to a boil. Add green onions, ginger, and star anise; bring to a boil. Add chicken, breast side down, cover, and bring to a boil. Reduce heat to low, cover, and simmer for 40 minutes. Turn off heat and let stand, covered, for 20 minutes.

3. Combine Pepper Salt ingredients in a frying pan. Cook, stirring, over low heat, until toasted and fragrant, about 3 minutes. Let cool.

4. Drain chicken, reserving liquid for stock. Cut chicken into 2-inch pieces or carve, western-style. Serve with Pepper Salt.

Makes 4 to 6 servings

 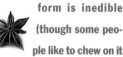

Lemon Chicken is one of the best-known and best-loved dishes served in Cantonese restaurants all over the world. This version, sweetened with honey and diced melon, was inspired by a memorable Lemon Chicken we were served at the restaurant of the Splendid China theme park in Shenzen in southern China.

HONEY-GLAZED LEMON CHICKEN

ZESTY TIPS

The zest is the outermost, colored layer of a citrus fruit, and that's where all the fragrant oils are. So when a recipe like this one calls for grated or shredded lemon zest, that's the part you want, not the white peel below it. If you don't have a lemon zester, use a grater, and cover it with a piece of kitchen parchment before grating. When you're done, the paper will peel right off and the zest won't be caught in the holes. Try it, it works! You can also shave off thin pieces of zest with a vegetable peeler, then stack them and slice them into fine shreds with a sharp knife.

4 boneless, skinless chicken breast halves

Marinade
2 tablespoons oyster flavored sauce
1 tablespoon cornstarch

Sauce
⅓ cup lemon juice
¼ cup honey
2 tablespoons chicken broth
2 teaspoons soy sauce
1 teaspoon grated lemon peel or orange peel
2 teaspoons cornstarch

Cooking oil for deep-frying
Cornstarch for dry-coating
1 egg, lightly beaten
¾ cup panko (Japanese-style bread crumbs)
½ cup diced honeydew melon
½ cup diced cantaloupe

Method
1. Place chicken pieces between 2 sheets of plastic wrap and pound lightly with flat side of a mallet until about ¼-inch thick. Combine marinade ingredients in a bowl. Add chicken and stir to coat. Let stand for 10 minutes. Combine sauce ingredients in a saucepan; set aside.

2. Heat oil in a wok to 350°F. Dredge chicken in cornstarch; shake to remove excess. Dip into egg, drain briefly, then coat with panko. Deep-fry chicken, turning once, and cook until golden brown, 3 to 4 minutes on each side. Remove and drain on paper towels.

3. Heat sauce over medium heat and cook, stirring, until sauce boils and thickens. Add honeydew melon and cantaloupe; cook until heated through.

4. To serve, cut chicken into bite-size pieces, arrange on a plate, and pour sauce over the top.

Makes 4 servings

This simple stir-fry combines four of the essential Chinese flavors—the sweetness of honey and lychee, the salty flavor of soy sauce and hoisin, the sour taste of lemon and the spiciness of chiles and garlic—with a hint of melon fragrance. No wonder it's so good!

HONEY-LYCHEE CHICKEN

¾ pound boneless, skinless chicken

Marinade
2 tablespoons oyster flavored sauce
    or soy sauce
2 teaspoons cornstarch

Sauce
¼ cup syrup from canned lychees
2 tablespoons lemon juice
2 tablespoons honey
1 tablespoon hoisin sauce
2 teaspoons soy sauce
1 teaspoon cornstarch

2 tablespoons cooking oil
6 to 8 small dried red chiles
1 teaspoon minced garlic
1 cup lychees
½ cup cantaloupe balls

Method
1. Cut chicken into 1-inch pieces. Combine marinade ingredients in a bowl. Add chicken and stir to coat. Let stand for 10 minutes. Combine sauce ingredients in a bowl; set aside.

2. Place a wok over high heat until hot. Add oil, swirling to coat sides. Add chiles, and garlic; cook, stirring, until fragrant, about 10 seconds.

3. Add chicken and stir-fry for 2 minutes. Add lychees, cantaloupe, and sauce; cook, stirring, until sauce boils and thickens.

Makes 4 servings

A re you ready to have a ball? These succulent "meatballs" of minced chicken with a crispy walnut coating are served in the kind of sweet and fruity sauce that Cantonese cooks love to pair with fried foods. The chicken balls, cantaloupe balls and lychees, all tumbled together on the plate, make an attractive presentation.

CHICKEN BALLS WITH LYCHEE SAUCE

¾ **pound boneless, skinless chicken**
1 **egg white, lightly beaten**
2 **tablespoons chicken broth**
1 **tablespoon rice wine or dry sherry**
1 **tablespoon cornstarch**
¾ **teaspoon salt**
¼ **teaspoon white pepper**
1 **cup finely chopped walnuts**

Sauce
1 **can (15 ounces) lychees,**
    undrained
1 **cup cantaloupe balls**
¼ **cup sweet chili sauce**
2 **tablespoons orange juice**

Cooking oil for deep-frying

Method

1. Cut chicken into 1-inch pieces. Place in a food processor and process until finely chopped. Add egg white, broth, wine, cornstarch, salt, and pepper. Process until mixture is smooth. Remove the chicken mixture to a bowl. Shape into balls, each about 1¼ inches in diameter. Roll balls in walnuts to coat evenly.

2. Drain lychees and pour ⅓ cup of their syrup into a saucepan. Add lychees, cantaloupe, sweet chili sauce, and orange juice; set aside.

3. Heat oil in a wok to 350°F. Deep-fry chicken balls, a few at a time, and cook, turning frequently, until centers of balls are opaque (cut a tiny slit to test), 7 minutes. Remove and drain on paper towels.

4. Heat sauce over medium heat and cook, stirring, until sauce is heated through. To serve, arrange chicken balls on a plate and pour sauce over the top.

Makes 4 servings

MELON MANIA

All over southern China, you'll find melons on the menu. But did you know they're as likely to be vegetables as fruits? The vegetable variety, which are actually gourds, must be cooked to be eaten—usually by steaming or in stews and soups. These include the huge green winter melon (sometimes carved and used as a soup tureen), the bumpy, green bitter melon (an acquired taste) and my favorite, the cute little fuzzy melon, which is covered with stubbly hair and has a delicate flavor and texture. Muskmelons (like cantaloupe) and watermelons are eaten as refreshments and are often used in cooking.

Crisp-skinned, succulent and delicious, Pei Pa Duck (named after the Chinese lute the flattened duck resembles) is to the South what Peking Duck is to the North.

CRISPY PEI PA ROAST DUCK

BEST OF DUCK

You often see flattened Pei Pa ducks hanging in the window of Cantonese delis and restaurants. What makes them so crispy and attractive? The secret is removing as much of the fat as possible before roasting. First, the duck is briefly parboiled, melting away some of the fat. To tighten the skin and allow more fat to drip out, the duck is then hung to air-dry. "Lacquering" the bird with a sweet glaze that caramelizes during roasting, also adds crispness and rich color.

1 duckling (4 to 5 pounds), cleaned

Marinade
2 teaspoons cooking oil
2 tablespoons minced ginger
1 tablespoon minced shallot
3 tablespoons hoisin sauce
2 tablespoons soy sauce
½ teaspoon Chinese five-spice

2 cups boiling water

Glaze
1½ cups water
¼ cup rice vinegar
¼ cup honey or maltose
¼ teaspoon red food coloring
     (optional)

Plum sauce

Method
1. Cut through breastbone of duck with poultry shears; spread duck open, skin side up, on a flat surface and press firmly to crack bones and flatten. Place duck, skin side down, on a rack in a roasting pan.

2. Prepare marinade: Place a saucepan over high heat until hot. Add oil, swirling to coat sides. Add ginger, and shallot; cook, stirring, until fragrant, about 10 seconds.

Remove saucepan from heat and stir in remaining marinade ingredients. Brush marinade over duck flesh. Refrigerate duck, uncovered, for 6 hours or overnight.

3. Turn duck on rack, skin side up. Pour boiling water over duck skin. Drain water from roasting pan. Let duck dry on rack for 30 minutes. Combine glaze ingredients in a saucepan and bring to a boil. Pour glaze over duck skin. Lift off duck and hang in a cool place until skin is taut and dry, 4 to 6 hours (2 hours if you use an electric fan.)

4. Preheat oven to 400°F. Place duck, skin side up, on a rack in a foil-lined roasting pan; roast, uncovered, for 40 minutes. Turn duck over, cover loosely with foil, and roast for 15 minutes. Turn duck skin side up again and brush with pan drippings. Place 5 to 6 inches below a preheated broiler; broil until skin is golden brown and crisp, 3 to 5 minutes.

5. Cut duck into serving size pieces and arrange on a serving plate. Serve with plum sauce on the side.

Makes 2 to 4 servings

Chinese cooks love to use the fresh and preserved forms of a single ingredient in the same dish, and this flavorful stir-fry is a perfect example. The combination of young ginger, candied ginger and pickled ginger make every bite a tasty surprise! If you can't find young ginger, substitute regular fresh ginger—though you may want to reduce the quantity slightly, to taste.

THREE GINGER BEEF

Marinade
2 tablespoons oyster flavored sauce
2 teaspoons cornstarch

³/₄ **pound flank steak, thinly sliced**

Sauce
2 tablespoons chopped red pickled
    ginger
1 tablespoon chopped crystallized
    ginger
¹/₄ **cup water**
1 ¹/₂ tablespoons plum sauce
1 tablespoon dark soy sauce
2 teaspoons sesame oil
¹/₂ **teaspoon sugar**

2 tablespoons cooking oil
2 tablespoons julienned young
    ginger
¹/₂ **cup pineapple chunks**
1 teaspoon cornstarch dissolved
    in 2 teaspoons water

Method
1. Combine marinade ingredients in a bowl. Add beef and stir to coat. Let stand for 10 minutes. Combine sauce ingredients in a bowl; set aside.

2. Place a wok over high heat until hot. Add oil, swirling to coat sides. Add beef and stir-fry until barely pink, about 2 minutes. Add young ginger and stir-fry for 30 seconds.

3. Add pineapple and sauce; bring to a boil. Add cornstarch solution and cook, stirring, until sauce boils and thickens.

Makes 4 servings

GINGERLY YOURS

Ginger is one of the oldest and most used ingredients in Chinese and Japanese cooking. The Chinese believe it can stimulate the appetite, suppress a cough, improve your memory and a lot of other things I can't quite remember! It has the amazing property of making foods like meat and fish taste fresher, even when they're a little over the hill. Hawaiian young ginger, available in summer, has a delicate flavor and a thin, pinkish skin that needs no peeling. Candied ginger, cooked and sugar-coated, has a strong, sweet-spicy bite. Red pickled ginger, cured in a salt, vinegar and sugar brine, is tangy and sweet.

115

*A*ttention beef-lovers. This one is for you! Wok-seared slices of tender steak in a robust brown sauce, with a colorful medley of sweet bell peppers.

TRIPLE PEPPER STEAK

1 pound flank steak, thinly sliced
   diagonally

Marinade
2 tablespoons oyster flavored sauce
2 teaspoons cornstarch
½ teaspoon black pepper

½ each green, red, and yellow
   bell pepper, julienned

Sauce
⅓ cup beef broth
2 tablespoons rice wine
   or dry sherry
2 tablespoons dark soy sauce
1 teaspoon cornstarch
1 teaspoon sugar
½ teaspoon black pepper

3 tablespoons cooking oil
2 tablespoons water
1 teaspoon minced garlic
½ teaspoon minced ginger
Jalapeño or serrano chili slices
   for garnish

Method

1. Combine marinade ingredients in a bowl. Add beef and stir to coat. Let stand for 10 minutes. Combine sauce ingredients in a bowl; set aside.

2. Place a wok over high heat until hot. Add 1 tablespoon oil, swirling to coat sides. Add bell peppers and stir-fry for 1 minute. Add water and stir-fry until bell peppers are crisp-tender, 2 to 3 minutes. Remove bell peppers to a serving plate.

3. Add remaining 2 tablespoons oil to wok, swirling to coat sides. Add beef and pan-fry until browned on both sides, but pink within, 1½ to 2 minutes on each side. Remove the beef from the wok.

4. Remove all but ½ teaspoon oil from wok. Add garlic and ginger; stir-fry until fragrant, about 10 seconds. Return beef to wok and add sauce; cook until sauce boils and thickens. Place beef over bell peppers and garnish with chili slices.

Makes 4 servings

PEPPER PREP

Here's an easy method chefs use for slicing bell peppers. Begin by cutting off the top and bottom of the pepper. Next, make a single cut along the side, to open the pepper. Pull out and discard the central core of membranes and seeds. Now lay the pepper skin-side down on a cutting board, spreading it out flat. Holding a sharp knife or cleaver flat against the pepper, trim away any remaining membrane. You now have a long flat rectangle that's easy to slice crosswise into uniform strips.

Broccoli Beef is another favorite in many Chinese restaurants in America. I think this version, made with two kinds of broccoli—the regular western kind and tender, sweet Chinese broccoli (gai lan)—is twice as good!

TWO BROCCOLI BEEF

GROWING YOUR OWN

Growing up with a garden in the back yard that fed our family all year long, I'm a great believer in gardening. It's relaxing and fun, and you get to enjoy fresher vegetables than you can find in any store. If you have a garden, try growing your own Chinese vegetables. Leafy green ones, like Chinese broccoli, bok choy and snow peas grow well during the early spring. Later in the spring, you can also plant warm-weather gourds, squashes and Chinese yard-long beans.

Marinade
2 tablespoons oyster flavored sauce
2 teaspoons dark soy sauce
2 teaspoons cornstarch

¾ pound flank steak, thinly sliced

Sauce
¼ cup water
3 tablespoons rice wine
    or dry sherry
2 tablespoons oyster flavored sauce
1 teaspoon dark soy sauce
1 teaspoon sesame oil
½ teaspoon chili paste
2 teaspoons cornstarch

½ pound Chinese broccoli,
    cut into bite-size pieces
2 cups regular broccoli florets
2 tablespoons cooking oil
2 teaspoons minced garlic
2 teaspoons minced ginger

Method
1. Combine marinade ingredients in a bowl. Add beef and stir to coat. Let stand for 10 minutes. Combine sauce ingredients in a bowl; set aside.

2. Parboil Chinese broccoli and broccoli florets separately in a pot of boiling water for 2 minutes. Drain, rinse with cold water, and drain again.

3. Place a wok over high heat until hot. Add oil, swirling to coats sides. Add garlic and ginger; cook, stirring, until fragrant, about 10 seconds. Add beef and stir-fry until barely pink, about 2 minutes. Add sauce and cook, stirring, until sauce boils and thickens.

4. To serve, place Chinese broccoli in the center of a serving plate. Spoon beef on top. Arrange broccoli florets in a circle around beef.

Makes 4 servings

Chinese broccoli (*gai lan*)

In the West, spareribs are usually barbecued or baked. In China, they're often steamed to tender, succulent perfection. These ribs are delicious both ways. If you prefer to bake them, coat them in the sauce, spread them in a single layer on a baking pan, cover the pan with foil and bake in a 350°F–375°F oven until tender, about 1 hour.

STEAMED SPARERIBS IN PLUM SAUCE

Sauce
1 piece (about 1½-inches square)
      dried tangerine peel
1 salted plum (optional)
2 teaspoons minced ginger
¼ cup plum sauce
2 tablespoons plum wine
2 teaspoons dark soy sauce
1 teaspoon sugar
1 tablespoon cornstarch

½ side (about 1 pound)
      pork spareribs, cut
      into 1½-inch pieces
Sliced plum for garnish

Method
1. Prepare sauce: Soak tangerine peel in warm water to cover until softened, about 15 minutes; drain. Finely chop tangerine peel. If using salted plum, soak in warm water to cover until softened, about 15 minutes; drain. Remove and discard seed; mash flesh. Combine tangerine peel and salted plum in a bowl. Add remaining sauce ingredients; set aside.

2. Add spareribs to sauce and stir to coat. Place spareribs and sauce in a heat-proof glass pie dish.

3. Prepare a wok for steaming (see page 29). Cover and steam spareribs over high heat, stirring once, until spareribs are tender, 40 to 45 minutes.

4. Place spareribs on a serving plate and garnish with sliced plums.

Makes 4 servings

SCHOOL OF HARD WOKS
I began my restaurant career at age 13 as an apprentice at the Sun Wong Kee restaurant in Kowloon, Hong Kong. In Chinese restaurant kitchens, the attitude is, "you have to crawl before you can wok," so I started out working the floor—with a broom and a scrub brush! Eventually, I graduated to prep cook and mastered the art of the lightning-fast cleaver. I worked 16-hour days in exchange for room and board. Literally. My bed was a narrow board that fit between two benches of a booth in the dining room!

Cantonese restaurants and delicatessens prepare a wonderful roasted pork specialty called "char siu"—strips of roast pork with a sweet red glaze—that's served hot or cold and sliced for use in soups, noodle dishes and dumpling fillings. The same preparation is used for mouth-watering pork spareribs. Here's an easy way to reproduce the effect at home using prepared char siu or hoisin sauce as a base for the marinade.

CHINESE BARBECUED SPARERIBS

HOISIN SAUCE

Like soy sauce and oyster sauce, hoisin sauce is one of those versatile pantry staples I always keep on hand. Made from fermented soybean paste, vinegar, garlic and sugar, and often seasoned with five-spice and a touch of chiles, it's served as a condiment for dishes like Peking Duck and Mu Shu Pork. As a marinade and basting sauce for grilled or roasted meats, it adds a sweet, tangy flavor and beautiful reddish-brown color. Try mixing it with your favorite bottled barbecue sauce to create your own "secret recipe."

1 side (2 to 2½ pounds) pork
    spareribs, trimmed of excess fat

Marinade
⅓ cup char siu sauce or hoisin sauce
3 tablespoons rice wine
    or dry sherry
3 tablespoons soy sauce
1 tablespoon sesame oil
1 tablespoon minced ginger
2 teaspoons minced garlic
1 teaspoon Chinese five-spice

Char siu sauce or hoisin sauce for
    basting

Method
1. Combine marinade ingredients in a bowl. Add spareribs and stir to coat. Cover and refrigerate for 4 to 6 hours or overnight.

2. Preheat oven to 400°F. Place spareribs on a rack in a foil-lined baking pan; cover loosely with foil. Bake for 30 minutes. Turn spareribs over, baste with char siu sauce, and continue baking, loosely covered, until tender, about 30 minutes.

3. Baste with char siu sauce again. Bake, uncovered, for 6 minutes. Turn spareribs over, baste with char siu sauce, and bake for 6 more minutes or until nicely glazed.

Makes 4 to 6 servings

This fluffy, pilaf-style rice, flavored with baby bok choy and ham, makes a colorful and substantial side dish. It tastes a bit like fried rice, but it's easier to make because you cook the raw rice together with all the other ingredients in a single pot.

HAM AND VEGETABLE RICE

HAM IT UP

Chinese cooks love to "ham it up" in the kitchen, and I'm no exception (in case you hadn't noticed!). The most famous Chinese ham comes from the southwestern province of Yunnan. It's cured and smoked, and can be eaten as is, though it's mostly used in cooked dishes. Yunnan ham is not exported to the West, where Chinese cooks often use Smithfield ham—a deep-red, highly flavored salted ham from Virginia—as a substitute. Italian prosciutto will also do the trick.

2 tablespoons cooking oil
2 teaspoons minced ginger
1 teaspoon minced garlic
2 ounces ham, chopped
4 Shanghai baby bok choy
   or baby bok choy, sliced
2 cups uncooked long-grain rice
3 cups chicken broth
1 tablespoon soy sauce or oyster
   flavored sauce
2 teaspoons sesame oil
2 teaspoons chopped cilantro

Method

1. Place a 2-quart pot over high heat until hot. Add cooking oil, swirling to coat sides. Add ginger and garlic; cook, stirring, until fragrant, about 10 seconds. Add ham and bok choy; stir-fry for 1 minute.

2. Add rice and mix well. Add broth and bring to a boil. Reduce heat to medium-high and cook, uncovered, until crater-like holes appear on rice.

3. Reduce heat to low, cover, and continue cooking until liquid is absorbed and rice is tender, 18 to 20 minutes.

4. Add soy sauce, sesame oil, and cilantro; mix well.

Makes 4 to 6 servings

Soup for dessert? Why not? After all, the Chinese serve sweet and savory soups throughout the meal. Halfway between a soup and a pudding, this tapioca dessert is wonderfully soothing when served warm, and light and refreshing when chilled. It gets its unusual creamy flavor from soy milk.

SWEET TAPIOCA CREAM SOUP

½ cup small (⅛-inch) pearl tapioca
1 cup cold water
2 cups soybean milk or regular milk
1 cup warm water
⅓ cup sugar
2 tablespoons minced crystallized
    ginger
2 egg yolks, lightly beaten
1 teaspoon vanilla extract
Mandarin orange slices for garnish

Method

1. Soak tapioca in cold water for 1 hour (most of water will be asorbed); drain.

2. Combine soy bean milk, warm water, sugar, and crystallized ginger in a heavy saucepan. Cook, stirring, over medium heat, until sugar dissolves.

Add tapioca and bring to a boil. Reduce heat to medium-low and cook, stirring, until mixture thickens and tapioca becomes translucent, about 15 minutes.

3. Combine egg yolks and vanilla extract in a bowl. Add ½ cup hot tapioca mixture; mix to combine. Return tapioca mixture back to saucepan and cook, stirring, for 1 minute.

4. Serve warm in individual bowls garnished with mandarin orange slices or let cool, cover, and refrigerate until chilled.

Makes 6 to 8 servings

TAPIOCA 101

When I think of tapioca, I always remember my first day at the Overseas Institute of Cookery in Hong Kong. Our teacher, a renowned master chef, began the class by holding up a cupful of tapioca starch and telling us: "Gentlemen, here you learn by observation. I am going to teach you how much tapioca starch to put in the food, how much to put in your uniforms, and how not to confuse the two. The rest, you must figure out for yourselves!"

In southern China, mangoes turn up in sweet soups and puddings like this one, made with creamy coconut milk. This molded pudding is easy to prepare ahead of time. For an elegant dinner party, I like to make it in individual ramekins, unmold them onto small plates and garnish with fresh tropical fruit.

MANGO PUDDING

2 mangoes, each about 12 ounces
1 ¼ cups cold water
2 packages (2 tablespoons) unflavored gelatin
⅔ cup sugar
½ cup regular milk
½ cup coconut milk
Sliced starfruit for garnish

Method

1. Peel mangoes and cut flesh from seeds. Cut mango into ¼-inch cubes to make ½ cup. Chop remaining mango to make about 1 ½ cups. Place in a blender with 1 cup cold water and puree until smooth.

2. Sprinkle gelatin over the remaining ¼ cup cold water in a bowl; let soften for several minutes.

3. Combine sugar and milk in a 2-quart saucepan. Cook, stirring, over medium-low heat, until sugar dissolves. Remove sugar mixture from heat; add softened gelatin and stir until dissolved.

4. Add coconut milk and mango puree; whisk until blended. Fold in diced mango. Pour into a 1 quart mold or divide among 5 individual 1-cup capacity ramekins or custard cups. Cover and refrigerate until firm, about 3 to 4 hours, or overnight.

5. To serve, warm base of mold in a bowl of warm water to loosen pudding. Place a serving plate over mold, then invert to unmold. Arrange sliced starfruit around pudding.

Makes 5 servings

Note: Shake the can of coconut milk before opening to mix the heavy coconut cream with the thin coconut milk.

"MILKING" A COCONUT

Did you know that the liquid that sloshes around inside a coconut isn't coconut milk? It's called coconut water. The milk and cream of a coconut are actually extracted from its meat. To make your own, chop the meat of a coconut in a food processor, then add a cup of hot water and puree. Press the coconut mixture through a fine sieve to extract the rich cream. Return the meat to the food processor blend with another cup of hot water, then strain again to extract the thinner milk. Coconut milk is an essential flavoring ingredient in most Asian cuisines.

What makes this steamed custard so creamy and silky, yet so light? Surprise! It's soft tofu, puréed until smooth in the food processor. The versatile soybean strikes again! I developed this recipe for a program on cooking with kids, and my pint-sized guest chefs gave it high marks.

LEMONY TOFU CUSTARD

2 slices white sandwich bread
1 package (16 ounces) soft tofu, drained
½ cup milk
3 eggs, lightly beaten
⅔ cup sugar
2 teaspoons grated lemon peel

Method

1. Trim and discard bread crusts. Cut center portion of bread into ½-inch cubes to make 1 cup.

2. Mash tofu in a bowl. Place tofu in a clean towel and squeeze to remove excess liquid. Place in a food processor and process until tofu is smooth. Add bread, milk, eggs, and sugar. Process until smooth.

3. Stir in lemon peel and mix well.

4. Pour tofu mixture into 4 to 6 individual 1-cup capacity ramekins or custard cups. Prepare a wok for steaming (see page 29).

5. Cover and steam custard over a gentle boil until a knife inserted in center comes out clean, about 15 minutes. Remove ramekins from steamer and let cool for 1 hour.

Makes 4 to 6 servings

YOUNG AT HEART

Wherever I travel, I love to take time to kid around with kids. Their innocence and happiness inspires me and keeps me feeling young. In China, I'm always struck by the way children are taught to respect their elders—you have to when you have several generations all living in close quarters under one roof. I hope I can give my own kids the precious gift of family connection that my parents and my homeland gave me.

It's not every day that kids see a passing TV crew on the road to Foshan.

Few desserts are this easy, this healthy and this beautiful. The "custard," in reality, is simply cubes of chilled soft tofu. But when it's topped with a lemon syrup and a colorful array of berries and tropical fruits, it tastes creamy, silky and refreshingly light. You can use just about any fresh or canned fruit, from orange, grapefruit and mandarin orange sections to pineapple, papaya and mango.

TOFU CUSTARD WITH TROPICAL FRUITS

1 ½ **cups water**
⅔ **cup crushed rock sugar or honey**
2 **tablespoons lemon juice**
½ **cup jackfruit chunks**
½ **cup each longans and loquats**
½ **cup raspberries or blueberries**
½ **cup diced cantaloupe**
2 **packages (16 ounces each) soft
    tofu, drained**

Method

1. Combine water, rock sugar, and lemon juice in a non-reactive saucepan. Cook, stirring occasionally, over low heat until sugar dissolves, 6 to 8 minutes. Remove saucepan from heat and add all fruit. Let cool; cover and refrigerate until chilled.

2. Cut tofu into ½-inch cubes and place in a serving bowl. Spoon fruit and syrup over tofu. Serve chilled.

Makes 8 servings

THE TOPIC IS TROPICAL

The longan, also known as "dragon's eye," looks like a lychee, small and round with a smooth brown shell. In the West, I've seen fresh ones in Asian markets during the summer, and they're sold in cans year-round. The loquat originated in China and looks and tastes like a cross between an apricot and a plum. Canned loquats are easier to find than fresh ones. The gigantic jackfruit is a sweet tropical fruit that grows to weights of up to 100 pounds! In the U.S., it's sold only in cans.

Shanghai~Where the

At the mouth of the mighty Yangtze River lies Shanghai, the sprawling eastern seaport that is China's largest city. A city of infinite mystery and cosmopolitan style, it's been called "The Paris of the East." Personally, I like to call Paris "The Shanghai of the West!" Shanghai is the culinary capital of eastern China, a region known for its mild weather, and abundant freshwater fish and shellfish, seafood, produce,

River Meets the Sea.

rice and tea. Exquisite presentations and complex sauces, often sweetened with sugar and seasoned with dark soy sauce, are the hallmarks of Shanghainese cooking, as well as slow-simmered soups and stews of pork and poultry. Rice wine from Shao Hsing, China's wine capital, is a prominent ingredient here, along with vinegar from Zhejiang and ham from Jinhua.

When Marco Polo visited Hangzhou and the West Lake in the 12th century, he called it an earthly paradise. It's still one of the most picturesque places in China, surrounded by lush green hills and beautiful pavilions and temples. We were served a version of this fresh, simple beef soup at an elegant banquet on the West Lake.

WEST LAKE BEEF SOUP

A FLOATING FEAST

I'll never forget the exquisite banquet prepared for us by 14 master chefs aboard a houseboat in the middle of the West Lake. Each chef created two Shanghainese specialties, including freshwater bass from the lake, served in a crab and milk sauce (Shanghai is one of the few areas in China where milk is used in cooking); succulent "red cooked pork," braised in wine, sugar and soy sauce; prawns cooked in Dragon Well tea; and shellfish steamed in orange "baskets."

Marinade
3 tablespoons water
2 tablespoons rice wine
   or dry sherry
1 tablespoon cornstarch

½ pound lean ground beef
5 cups beef broth
2 tablespoons regular soy sauce
1 tablespoon dark soy sauce
½ teaspoon white pepper
½ leek (white part only), julienned
⅓ cup frozen peas, thawed
¼ cup diced carrots
1 tablespoon chopped cilantro
3 tablespoons cornstarch dissolved
   in ¼ cup water
2 egg whites, lightly beaten
1 teaspoon sesame oil

Method
1. Combine marinade ingredients in a bowl. Add beef and mix well. Let stand for 10 minutes.

2. Place broth, soy sauces, and pepper in a 2-quart pot; bring to a boil. Add beef and stir to separate. Add leek, peas, carrots, and cilantro. Reduce heat to low and simmer for 5 minutes.

3. Add cornstarch solution and cook, stirring, until soup boils and thickens. Turn off heat. Add egg whites, stirring, until they form long threads. Stir in sesame oil.

Makes 4 to 6 servings

These golden croquettes, coated in sesame seeds and wrapped in a band of seaweed, make an attractive and unusual appetizer. Give each guest a little dish of spiced "pepper-salt" on the side for dipping.

NORI TOFU ROLLS

¼ cup finely diced carrots
1 sheet Japanese seaweed *(nori)*
1 package (14 ounces) extra-firm
    tofu, drained
¼ cup finely diced red bell pepper
1 green onion, finely chopped
1 tablespoon cornstarch
¾ teaspoon salt
¼ teaspoon white pepper
1 egg white, lightly beaten
½ cup sesame seeds
3 tablespoons cooking oil
Pepper Salt (see page 109)

Method
1. Parboil carrots in a pot of boiling water for 2 minutes; drain. Cut seaweed into 6 strips, each about ¾-inch wide.

2. Mash tofu in a bowl. Place tofu in a clean towel and squeeze to remove excess liquid. Return to bowl and add carrots, bell pepper, green onion, cornstarch, salt, pepper, and ½ of the egg white (1 tablespoon); mix well.

3. Divide tofu mixture into 6 portions. With oiled hands, roll each portion into a cylinder about 3-inches long and 1-inch wide. Roll each cylinder in sesame seeds, lightly press to coat.

4. Wrap a strip of seaweed around the middle; brush edges with remaining egg white and press to seal. Gently flatten roll to make a rectangle about ½-inch thick.

5. Place a wide frying pan over high heat until hot. Add oil, swirling to coat sides. Add rolls and pan-fry, turning once, until golden brown, about 2 minutes on each side.

6. Remove and drain on paper towels. Serve hot with Pepper Salt on the side.

Makes 6

NORI NOTE

In Shanghai, and along the eastern coast of China, seaweed is a popular ingredient in cooking. In the U.S., it's sold under its Japanese name, *nori*, and mostly used for making sushi. I love to use a ribbon of nori as a wrapper for fried dishes like this one, because it adds an artful stripe of color, a little textural interest and a savory, oceany flavor.

At a charming teahouse in a garden in Souzhou, we were served tender pork-filled dumplings like these, lightly steamed and served Shanghai-style with wine vinegar and ginger.

STEAMED SHANGHAI BUNS

2½ **cups all-purpose flour**
½ **cup boiling water**
⅔ **cup cold water**

Filling
¾ **pound lean ground pork, beef, or chicken**
⅔ **cup chicken broth**
3 **tablespoons finely chopped onions**
2 **tablespoons oyster flavored sauce**
2 **teaspoons soy sauce**
2 **teaspoons sesame oil**

Dipping Sauce
¼ **cup red wine vinegar**
2 **teaspoons shredded ginger**

Method
1. Place flour in a bowl. Add boiling water, stirring with chopsticks or a fork. Gradually stir in cold water, mixing until dough holds together. On a lightly floured board, knead dough until smooth and satiny, about 5 minutes. Cover and let rest for 30 minutes.

2. Combine filling ingredients in a bowl; mix well. Combine red wine vinegar and ginger in a bowl; set aside.

3. On a lightly floured board, roll dough into a cylinder, then cut into 28 portions. To make each bun, roll a portion of dough into a 4-inch circle about ⅛-inch thick; keep remaining dough covered to prevent drying. Place a rounded tablespoon of filling in center of dough. Gather edges of dough around filling; pinch and pleat to seal.

4. Place buns, one half at a time, seam side up, in a heat-proof glass pie dish. Let buns rest for at least 5 minutes before steaming. Prepare a wok for steaming (see page 29).

5. Cover and steam buns over high heat, 8 to 10 minutes.

6. Remove to a serving plate and serve with dipping sauce on the side.

Makes 28

DUMPLING DOUGH

Why are some Chinese doughs made with boiling water? Because it heats and stretches the starch granules in the flour, allowing them to hold more water. This kind of "hot-water dough" is quite tender and is used to make the kind of chewy wrappers used in dumplings like *siu mai* and potstickers. Of course, you can also buy prepared siu mai or potsticker wrappers, but homemade hot-water dough is easy to make and has a wonderfully elastic texture.

The root of the lotus flower grows up to three feet long, and looks like a chain of potato-shaped pods. Once cooked, it has a firm texture and a mild sweet flavor that tastes mysteriously like a cross between a potato, a coconut and a water chestnut.

LOTUS ROOT WITH SEASONAL VEGETABLES

LAND OF THE LOTUS EATERS

The beautiful lotus flowers that grace the surface of many lakes and ponds in China are more than just decorative. The entire lotus plant is also a versatile cooking ingredient. The root, with its lacy pattern of Swiss-cheese-like holes, is used in vegetable and meat dishes or candied and eaten as a sweet. The seeds are eaten fresh or dried as a snack and also ground into a paste that's used in desserts and pastry fillings. And the leaves are used to wrap foods for steaming.

Sauce
2 tablespoons oyster flavored sauce
1 tablespoon soy sauce
2 teaspoons rice wine or dry sherry
1 teaspoon sesame oil

1 tablespoon cooking oil
½ pound lotus root, peeled and cut into ¼-inch thick slices
1 can (5 ounces) sliced water chestnuts, drained
1 cup broccoli florets
½ cup vegetable broth
¼ pound sugar snap peas, trimmed
½ red bell pepper, cut into 1-inch squares

Method
1. Combine sauce ingredients in a bowl; set aside.

2. Place a wok over high heat until hot. Add oil, swirling to coat sides. Add lotus root, water chestnuts, and broccoli; stir-fry for 30 seconds.

3. Add broth, cover, and cook for 3 minutes. Add sugar snap peas and bell pepper; stir-fry until vegetables are crisp-tender, 1 to 2 minutes. Add sauce and cook until heated through.

Makes 4 to 6 servings

Floating among the lotus flowers on the West Lake.

Here's a way to turn humble, unpretentious tofu into a work of art: a mosaic of tofu slices topped with vegetable flowers, pan-fried until crispy on the bottom, and served in a light sauce.

TOFU MOSAIC

1 package (16 ounces) soft
    or regular-firm tofu, drained

Sauce
⅓ cup vegetable broth
1 tablespoon soy sauce
1 tablespoon rice wine or dry sherry
½ teaspoon sesame oil
1 teaspoon sugar
¾ teaspoon cornstarch

¼ teaspoon cayenne
¼ teaspoon salt
¼ teaspoon white pepper
8 vegetable flowers
    or cut-outs (see column at right)
2 tablespoons cooking oil
1 egg, lightly beaten
All-purpose flour for dry-coating
Black sesame seeds for garnish

Method
1. Cut tofu in half horizontally to make 2 pieces, each about ¾-inch thick. Cut each half into quarters to make a total of 8 rectangles. Combine sauce ingredients in a saucepan; set aside.

2. Bring a pot of water to a simmer. Add tofu and parboil for 2 minutes. Lift out with a slotted spoon; pat dry with paper towels. Combine cayenne, salt, and white pepper in a bowl. Sprinkle cayenne mixture over tofu. Place a vegetable flower on top of each piece of tofu.

3. Place a wide non-stick frying pan over medium heat until hot. Add oil, swirling to coat sides. Dip bottom of tofu pieces in egg, drain briefly, then dredge in flour. Place in pan, coated side down, and cook until golden brown and crispy on the bottom, 2 to 3 minutes. Remove and drain on paper towels.

4. Heat sauce over medium heat and cook, stirring, until sauce boils and thickens. Pour sauce on a serving plate. Arrange tofu pieces on top of sauce and garnish with sesame seeds.

Makes 4 to 6 servings

VEGETABLE ART

The Chinese love to carve vegetables as fancy garnishes for festive occasions. To make delicate vegetable butterflies or flowers, cut thin slices of carrot, daikon, or radish or squares of bell pepper; use fancy canapé cutters (sold in kitchenware stores and also called aspic cutters) to stamp out shapes. Or use a paring knife or a fine wood chisel to cut notches along the length of a whole carrot, then cut thin crosswise slices. Voilà! Carrot flowers!

I've always been a lover of lotus root—its flavor, texture and beautiful appearance. Here, I've used it in a bright, fresh vegetable stir-fry with typically Shanghainese flavor accents: wine, soy sauce and sugar. For a special presentation try cutting vegetables into fancy shapes as shown at right.

MIXED VEGETABLE STIR-FRY

READY, SET, COOK!

Chinese cooking is easier when you do what experienced chefs do: take the time to set up your "station" in advance so there are no last-minute surprises. Cut up everything ahead of time. Soak dried ingredients. Marinate meats. Measure out ingredients and place them in small bowls. Group everything you'll need for each recipe on a separate tray, and set cooking utensils and pans within easy reach. Remember: "When the prep is well done, the cooking's more fun!"

Sauce
½ cup vegetable broth
1 tablespoon rice wine or dry sherry
1 tablespoon soy sauce
1 teaspoon sesame oil
2 teaspoons sugar
2 teaspoons cornstarch

1 tablespoon cooking oil
½ teaspoon minced garlic
½ teaspoon minced ginger
½ cup sliced carrots
½ cup sliced lotus root
½ cup sliced jícama
½ cup sliced zucchini
½ cup mushroom
2 tablespoons water
½ red bell pepper, cut into 1-inch
   squares
4 asparagus spears, trimmed and
   thinly sliced diagonally

Method
1. Combine sauce ingredients in a bowl; set aside.

2. Place a wok over high heat until hot. Add oil, swirling to coat sides. Add garlic, and ginger; cook, stirring until fragrant, about 10 seconds. Add carrots, lotus root, jícama, and zucchini and mushrooms; stir-fry for 1 minute.

3. Add water, cover, and cook for 3 minutes. Add bell pepper and asparagus; stir-fry for 1 minute. Add sauce and cook, stirring, until sauce boils and thickens.

Makes 4 servings

In China, eating a fish is like flipping a coin: heads or tails, you're always a winner. Chinese chefs know that the head and tail of a fish contain some of the juiciest and most flavorful bits of meat, and this Shanghai-style recipe is delicious proof. Ask your fish market to save you a tail from any medium-sized fish, such as cod, sea bass or red snapper. You can also make this recipe using fish fillets.

FISH TAIL IN BROWN SAUCE

POSTCARD FROM SHANGHAI

I'm sitting in a café on the busy waterfront boulevard known in Shanghai as the Bund. It's sunset, and the Parisian-style street lamps, a reminder of the city's colonial past, have just come on. Everyone's out tonight, families, sailors, couples strolling hand in hand along the waterfront. Behind me are the art-deco buildings of old Shanghai, and across the river, is Pudong, the futuristic metropolis that will soon be Asia's #1 sky-scraper city. I can see why they call Shanghai the "Crossroads of the East."

1 fish tail (about 1½ pounds),
    cleaned and scaled

Marinade
3 tablespoons soy sauce
¼ teaspoon white pepper

Sauce
4 slices ginger, julienned
¾ cup chicken broth
3 tablespoons Shao Hsing wine
2 tablespoons dark soy sauce
1 teaspoon sesame oil
1½ tablespoons sugar
¼ teaspoon white pepper

3 tablespoons cooking oil

Cornstarch for dry-coating

1 green onion, cut into 2-inch pieces
1 stalk lemongrass (bottom 6 inches
    only), sliced
1 teaspoon cornstarch dissolved in
    2 teaspoons water (optional)

Method
1. Cut fish lengthwise in 1-inch wide strips, leaving strips attached at the tail. Combine marinade ingredients in a bowl. Add fish and stir to coat. Let stand for 10 minutes. Combine sauce ingredients in a bowl; set aside.

2. Place a wide frying pan over high heat until hot. Add oil, swirling to coat sides. Dust fish with cornstarch; shake to remove excess.

3. Add fish and cook, turning once, until golden brown, about 2 minutes on each side. Add sauce, green onion, and lemongrass; bring to a boil.

4. Reduce heat to medium-low, cover, and simmer until fish turns opaque, 5 to 6 minutes. If desired, add cornstarch solution and cook, stirring, until sauce boils and thickens.

Makes 4 servings

When I was a child, my mom used to make a wonderful dish of lotus root slices coated with a flavorful ground pork stuffing. This is the Shanghainese version of that same home-style dish, stuffed with a purée of fish, such as salmon, lightly breaded and pan-fried until golden brown.

LOTUS SALMON PATTY

¼ **pound skinless salmon fillets, each about 1-inch thick**

Marinade
1 egg white, lightly beaten
1 tablespoon oyster flavored sauce
1 tablespoon rice wine or dry sherry
1 ½ tablespoons cornstarch
½ teaspoon salt
¼ teaspoon white pepper

¼ **cup finely chopped water chestnuts**
2 tablespoons minced ham
¾ **pound lotus root, peeled and cut into ¼-inch thick slices**
Cornstarch for dry-coating
1 egg, lightly beaten
¾ **cup panko (Japanese-style bread crumbs)**
3 tablespoons cooking oil

Method

1. Cut salmon into 1-inch pieces. Place in a food processor and process until finely chopped. Add marinade ingredients. Process until mixture is smooth. Remove the salmon mixture to a bowl. Add water chestnuts and ham; mix well. Let stand for 10 minutes.

2. To make each patty, dust a lotus root slice with cornstarch. Use ¼ cup fish mixture to cover both sides of lotus root. Dip patty in egg, drain briefly, then coat with panko.

3. Place a wide frying pan over medium heat until hot. Add oil, swirling to coat sides. Add patties and cook until golden brown, 2 to 3 minutes per side.

Makes 4 to 8 servings

IN PRAISE OF PANKO

If you like to make breaded, fried foods, there's no better coating than Japanese-style *panko* breadcrumbs. They're larger than western-style crumbs, with irregular shapes and sizes, a crispy texture and a lightly toasted flavor. Panko seem to absorb less grease than ordinary breadcrumbs, and they stay crunchy even after standing. If you can't find Panko in your grocery's Asian foods section, make your own crumbs from crackers or stale, crusty bread.

West Lake Fish is a popular Chinese restaurant dish that's served all over the world. This healthful version is poached whole and served with a Shanghai-style sweet and sour sauce that gets its appetizing, rich fragrance from vinegar, wine and a touch of brown sugar. Fish fillets can be substituted for the whole fish.

CLEAR-SIMMERED WEST LAKE FISH

BLACK VINEGAR

To the south of Shanghai is the central coast province of Zhejiang, which is famous in Chinese food circles for its aged black vinegar—a delightfully sweet-smoky condiment made from fermented rice, wheat and millet or sorghum. You may see it sold in Chinese markets as "Chinkiang Vinegar." If you can't find it, don't be sour: balsamic vinegar makes a good substitute, though you may want to reduce the amount of sugar in your recipe.

Sauce
6 tablespoons black vinegar
    or balsamic vinegar
2 tablespoons rice wine
    or dry sherry
1 tablespoon regular soy sauce
1 tablespoon dark soy sauce
2 teaspoons sesame oil
1 teaspoon chili sauce
3 tablespoons packed brown sugar

1 whole fish (1½ to 2 pounds),
    such as sea bass or red snapper,
    cleaned and scaled
6 slices ginger, lightly crushed
3 green onions, lightly crushed
1 teaspoon salt

Method
1. Combine sauce ingredients in a saucepan; set aside. Cut a slit, ¾-inch deep, along either side of dorsal fin.

2. Pour 2 inches of water into a wok or pan large enough to hold the fish. Add the ginger, green onions, and salt; bring to a boil.

3. Add fish, reduce heat to low, cover, and simmer until the fish turns opaque, 8 to 10 minutes. Remove fish from wok and place on a serving plate.

4. Heat sauce over low heat and cook, stirring, until sauce is heated through. Pour sauce over the top of fish.

Makes 4 to 6 servings

Note: Cooking time will vary depending on thickness of fish.

Here's my interpretation of a famous dish from Shao Hsing, China's rice wine capital: Fresh-water Drunken Crab. If the idea of cooking a live crab doesn't appeal to you, you can make this dish with cooked crab in the shell omitting the first step of the recipe.

DRUNKEN CRAB WITH GINGER-WINE SAUCE

4 live blue shell crabs or 1 live
    Dungeness crab

Sauce
½ cup chicken broth
⅓ cup Shao Hsing wine
2 tablespoons oyster flavored sauce
2 tablespoons soy sauce
1 teaspoon chili garlic sauce

½ cup all-purpose flour
3 tablespoons cooking oil
8 slices ginger, lightly crushed
6 green onions, sliced
¼ cup whole fresh basil leaves
1 teaspoon cornstarch dissolved
    in 2 teaspoons water (optional)

Method
1. Parboil crabs in a pot of boiling water for 2 minutes. Drain, rinse with cold water, and drain again. Clean crabs. Twist off claws and legs. Cut blue shell crab bodies in half; if using Dungeness crab, cut body into 4 pieces. Combine sauce ingredients in a bowl; set aside.

2. Dust crab pieces with flour. Place a wok over high heat until hot. Add oil, swirling to coat sides. Add crab and stir-fry for 1 minute. Add ginger and green onions; cook for 2 minutes. Add sauce and basil; bring to a boil. Reduce heat to low, cover, and simmer, stirring once or twice, until crab is cooked, 8 to 10 minutes.

3. Uncover and cook 1 or 2 minutes to reduce sauce, or add cornstarch solution and cook, stirring, until sauce boils and thickens.

Makes 4 servings

DRUNKEN DISHES

At one of Shao Hsing's most famous wine bars, we sat in the garden, drinking bowls of Shao Hsing wine, and feasting on an amazing variety of "drunken" dishes, from chicken and duck to fish and even octopus. My favorite is the legendary Drunken Freshwater Crab, kept alive in wine for three days before it's cooked. At least you know the crab died happy! You have to watch your step eating in Shao Hsing, or you may experience another local specialty: Drunken Guests!

Rice being poured into steaming vats at Shao Hsing.

Leaving the shell on these quickly stir-fried prawns steeped in a tangy wine sauce gives them extra flavor, but if you don't want the bother of having to remove the shells at the table, you can prepare this dish with shelled prawns, too.

SHAO HSING SAVORY PRAWNS

WINE OF THE TIMES

The rituals surrounding wine in China are ancient and fascinating. "Scholar's Wine" was buried underground by a father upon the birth of his first son, then unearthed years later and drunk in celebration of the son's graduation from college. "Bride's Wine" was buried at the birth of a daughter and drunk at her wedding. And "Withered Flower" wine was served at the death of a child to ensure peace in the next life.

½ pound medium raw prawns in
   the shell
1 tablespoon cornstarch
½ teaspoon salt

Sauce
⅓ cup Shao Hsing wine
3 tablespoons ketchup
2 tablespoons soy sauce
2 tablespoons rice vinegar
1 teaspoon sesame oil
1 teaspoon chili sauce
2 teaspoons sugar

2 tablespoons cooking oil
Chopped green onions for garnish

Method
1. Remove legs from prawns. If desired, cut through back of shells with scissors to remove sand vein. Combine cornstarch and salt in a bowl. Add prawns and stir to coat. Let stand for 10 minutes. Combine sauce ingredients in a bowl; set aside.

2. Place a wok over high heat until hot. Add oil, swirling to coat sides. Add prawns and stir-fry until prawns turn pink, 1 to 2 minutes. Add sauce and bring to a boil. Reduce heat to low and simmer for 5 minutes.

3. Remove to a serving plate and garnish with chopped green onions.

Makes 4 servings

Tea lends its richly aromatic flavor to dishes throughout eastern China, and shrimp, stir-fried with the tips of Dragon Well green tea leaves, is perhaps the most famous of them all. If Dragon Well tea is unavailable, substitute any high-quality green tea.

DRAGON WELL SHRIMP

ALL THE TEA IN CHINA

The Chinese drink three main types of tea: green tea, made from fresh leaves that are steamed and dried; black tea, made from leaves that are fully fermented before drying; and oolong tea, made from partially fermented leaves. China's most prized—and most pricey—green tea is grown at the Dragon Well Tea Farm in Hangzhou, nestled in a fertile valley between high mountains. Starting in early spring, the choicest tips are hand-picked, dried and sold to connoisseurs throughout the world.

At the Dragon Well Tea Farm, tea is carefully harvested by hand.

Marinade
½ egg white (1 tablespoon), lightly beaten
1 tablespoon cornstarch
½ teaspoon salt

¾ pound small to medium raw shrimp, shelled and deveined
½ cup boiling water
1 tablespoon Dragon Well tea leaves
1 tablespoon rice wine or dry sherry
¾ teaspoon sesame oil
⅛ teaspoon white pepper
2 tablespoons cooking oil
1 teaspoon minced ginger

Method

1. Combine marinade ingredients in a bowl. Add shrimp and stir to coat. Let stand for 10 minutes.

2. Combine boiling water and tea leaves in a bowl; let steep for 10 minutes.

3. Strain ¼ cup of the liquid tea in another bowl and add wine, sesame oil, and pepper. Reserve 1 tablespoon of the rehydrated tea leaves; discard remaining liquid tea and tea leaves.

4. Place a wok over high heat until hot. Add cooking oil, swirling to coat sides. Add ginger and cook, stirring, until fragrant, about 10 seconds.

5. Add shrimp and rehydrated tea leaves; stir-fry for 1½ minutes. Add liquid tea mixture and cook until sauce is heated through.

Makes 4 servings

144

Stir-fried shrimp in a creamy honey-lemon sauce make a wonderful textural contrast with crunchy candied walnuts in this contemporary Chinese restaurant-style dish.

HONEY WALNUT PRAWNS

Marinade
2 teaspoons cornstarch
¼ teaspoon salt
¼ teaspoon white pepper

¾ pound medium raw prawns,
    shelled and deveined

Sauce
⅓ cup mayonnaise
1 tablespoon honey
1 teaspoon soy sauce
⅓ teaspoon sesame oil

2 tablespoons walnut oil
2 tablespoons sugar
½ cup walnut halves
2 tablespoons cooking oil
1 teaspoon grated lemon peel
½ cup lychees
½ cup cantaloupe balls

Method
1. Combine marinade ingredients in a bowl. Add prawns and stir to coat. Let stand for 10 minutes. Combine sauce ingredients in a bowl; set aside.

2. Place a wide frying pan over medium heat until hot. Add walnut oil, swirling to coat sides. Add sugar and stir until it dissolves.

3. Add walnuts and stir until walnuts are coated with caramelized sugar. Immediately transfer to a foil-covered plate; separate walnuts with two forks.

4. Place a wok over high heat until hot. Add cooking oil, swirling to coat sides. Add prawns and lemon peel; stir-fry until prawns turn pink, 2 to 3 minutes.

5. Add sauce, lychees, and cantaloupe; cook for 1 minute. Place on a serving plate and garnish with candied walnuts.

Makes 4 servings

EAST-WEST EATS

Mayonnaise, in Chinese food? Why not? Honey Walnut Prawns is a perfect example of a new kind of cross-cultural Chinese cooking that's particularly popular in restaurants in Shanghai, Canton, and Hong Kong—cosmopolitan centers where western influences are most likely to take root first. You'll find ingredients like mayonnaise, Worcestershire sauce, and ketchup (which, by the way, originated in Malaysia in the first place!) being used to create new dishes that blend the best of East and West.

At the home of a family in Souzhou, my crew almost came to blows over who got seconds of this sweet and succulent braised pork dish.

SUZHOU BRAISED PORK IN A CLAY POT

1 ¼ pounds boneless pork shoulder

Marinade
2 tablespoons regular soy sauce
1 tablespoon dark soy sauce
1 tablespoon cornstarch

Broth
2 cups chicken broth
⅓ cup rice wine or dry sherry
2 tablespoons oyster flavored sauce
　　or regular soy sauce
2 tablespoon dark soy sauce
4 green onions, cut in half and
　　lightly crushed
2 whole star anise
1 cinnamon stick
¼ cup crushed rock sugar or
　　packed brown sugar

2 tablespoons cooking oil
6 cloves garlic, thinly sliced
½ pound napa cabbage, cut
　　into 1 ½-inch squares
1 ½ teaspoons cornstarch dissolved
　　in 1 tablespoon water

Method

1. Cut pork into 2-inch pieces. Combine marinade ingredients in a bowl. Add pork and stir to coat. Let stand for 10 minutes. Combine seasoning broth ingredients in a bowl.

2. Place a wok over high heat until hot. Add oil, swirling to coat sides. Add garlic and cook, stirring, until fragrant, about 10 seconds. Add pork and cook until browned on all sides, 3 to 4 minutes.

3. Place pork in a clay pot or a 2-quart pot. Add seasoning broth ingredients; bring to a boil over medium heat. Reduce heat to low, cover, and simmer until meat is tender, about 1 ¼ hours. Add cabbage, cover, and simmer until cabbage is crisp-tender, about 10 minutes. Add cornstarch solution and cook, stirring, until sauce boils and thickens.

4. To serve, place cabbage on a plate. Arrange pork over cabbage. Pour thickened sauce over the top.

Makes 4 to 6 servings

SUZHOU

Criss-crossed by picturesque canals and bridges, the ancient city of Souzhou in Jiangsu province, to the north of Shanghai, has been called "The Venice of the East." Since the time of the ancient silk road, China has been the world's largest producer of silk. And to this day, Souzhou, which produces two-thirds of China's total silk output, remains the silk capital of the world. Embroidery is elevated to a fine art here, too; needleworkers often take several years to complete a single piece.

Like a French terrine, this elegant dish is unmolded to reveal layers of colorful vegetables and chicken. It can also be prepared in individual ramekins and unmolded onto small serving plates. Either way, it can be prepared ahead of time and steamed at the last minute.

TRI-COLOR CHICKEN AND VEGETABLE MOLD

SESAME OIL

Asian-style sesame oil has a deep amber color because it's extracted from toasted sesame seeds. Don't confuse it with the clear type sold in some natural foods stores, which has a completely different flavor. Because it burns easily and has a strong flavor and aroma, sesame oil is used sparingly, as a condiment and seasoning in marinades, sauces and dressings, rather than as a cooking oil. It's often sprinkled on foods at the end of the cooking process as a final flavor booster.

8 large dried black mushrooms
½ cup julienned carrots
2 bunches spinach, stems removed
1 cup shredded cooked chicken breast

Sauce
½ cup chicken broth
2 tablespoons oyster flavored sauce
1 teaspoon sesame oil
¼ teaspoon white pepper

2 teaspoons cornstarch dissolved in 1 tablespoon water

Method
1. Soak mushrooms in warm water to cover until softened, about 15 minutes; drain. Trim and discard stems. Thinly slice caps. Parboil carrots in a pot of boiling water for 1 minute; drain, rinse with cold water, and drain again. Parboil spinach for 2 minutes; drain, rinse with cold water, and drain again. Let cool, then squeeze spinach dry with your hands. Combine sauce ingredients in bowl; set aside.

2. To prepare mold, you will need a 3 to 4-cup heat-proof glass bowl, about 8 inches in diameter and 4 inches deep. Line sides of bowl with mushroom, carrots, and chicken as illustrated. Place spinach in bowl, pressing down to pack tightly. Pour sauce over spinach.

3. Prepare a wok for steaming (see page 29). Cover and steam mold over high heat for 10 minutes.

4. Remove mold and carefully tip to drain sauce into a saucepan. Place a serving plate over bowl, then invert to unmold. Bring sauce to a boil. Add just enough cornstarch solution so sauce lightly coats a spoon. Pour sauce over mold.

Makes 4 to 6 servings

A popular cold dish, drunken chicken is marinated in wine, cooked in a steamer and chilled. The wine and chicken juices gelatinize, forming a kind of flavorful "aspic" which is served over the moist, tender chicken slices.

DRUNKEN CHICKEN

6 boneless chicken thighs

Marinade
¼ cup Shao Hsing wine
1 tablespoon soy sauce
1 teaspoon sugar
¾ teaspoon salt

4 slices ginger, lightly crushed
1 green onion, cut in half and lightly crushed
1 cup Shao Hsing wine
1 teaspoon sugar

Method
1. Place chicken pieces between 2 sheets of plastic wrap and pound lightly with flat side of a mallet to an even thickness. Combine marinade ingredients in a heat-proof glass pie dish. Add chicken and stir to coat.

2. Let stand for 10 minutes. Place ginger and green onion on top of chicken.

3. Prepare a wok for steaming (see page 29). Cover and steam chicken over high heat until chicken is no longer pink, 10 to 12 minutes. Let cool.

4. Add wine and sugar to chicken and steaming juices; cover and refrigerate for 24 hours.

5. To serve, discard ginger and green onion. Cut chicken into thin slices; arrange on a plate with the gelatinized juice. Serve chilled.

Makes 4 to 6 servings

SHAO HSING WINE

The rice wine of Shao Hsing in Zhejiang province is renowned throughout the world, not only as an accompaniment to Chinese food, but also as a flavoring ingredient in cooking. It's made by a process that has remained unchanged for more than 2,000 years. In outdoor urns covered with seaweed mats, rice is fermented with local lake water and an ancient strain of yeast that has been cultivated for centuries. The process can't be rushed—the wine ages at least 18 months, and sometimes up to 100 years.

Shao Hsing wine fermenting in vats.

The name of this famous specialty of eastern China refers to the large size of the meatballs and to their "manes" of sliced cabbage. In this lighter version, I've replaced the traditional added pork fat with tofu.

LION'S HEAD MEATBALLS

CILANTRO

Also known as fresh coriander or Chinese parsley, fresh cilantro has a distinctive aromatic flavor that people either love or can't stand. But once it's cooked, it has a less pronounced taste that marries well with fish, poultry and red meat. I like to use it as a garnish—placing a few leaves at one side of a serving platter, or floating individual sprigs on bowls of soup—because its soft, lacy leaves are so attractive. That way, guests can either eat it or set it aside.

6 dried black mushrooms

Meatballs
¼ **pound regular-firm tofu, drained**
¾ **pound lean ground pork or beef**
1 **egg, lightly beaten**
2 **tablespoons oyster flavored sauce**
2 **tablespoons cornstarch**
2 **teaspoons minced ginger**
2 **teaspoons minced cilantro**

Cooking oil for deep-frying
1½ **cups chicken broth**
2 **tablespoons rice wine**
    or dry sherry
1 **tablespoon soy sauce**
¾ **pound napa cabbage,**
    cut into 3-inch sections
1 **small carrot, thinly sliced**
    diagonally
16 **snow peas, trimmed and cut in**
    half diagonally
1 **teaspoon sesame oil**

Method
1. Soak mushrooms in warm water to cover until softened, about 15 minutes; drain. Trim and discard stems. Quarter caps.

2. Prepare meatballs: Mash tofu in a bowl. Place tofu in a clean towel and squeeze to extract liquid. Return to bowl and add remaining meatball ingredients; mix well. Divide mixture into 12 to 14 portions. Roll each portion into a ball.

3. Heat cooking oil in a wok to 350°F. Deep-fry meatballs, one half at a time, and cook, turning frequently, until browned on all sides, 3 to 4 minutes. Remove and drain on paper towels.

4. Place meatballs in a 2-quart pot. Add broth, wine, and soy sauce. Heat to simmering over medium heat. Cover and cook for 10 minutes.

5. Add mushrooms, cabbage, and carrot; cover and simmer for 10 more minutes. Add snow peas and simmer until they are crisp-tender, 2 to 3 minutes. Stir in sesame oil.

Makes 4 to 6 servings

The flavors of tea and rice are often combined in Chinese cooking, especially in Shanghai, where both are plentiful. This recipe is based on the Shanghainese method of cooking rice and vegetables together in the same pot. For a fancier presentation, spoon the cooked rice into custard cups or small bowls, unmold onto serving plates and top each serving with chopped toasted walnuts.

MUSHROOM TEA RICE

3 dried black mushrooms
1 cup boiling water
3 tablespoons oolong or Japanese
　　green tea leaves

Sauce
2 tablespoons oyster flavored sauce
2 teaspoons soy sauce

1 tablespoon cooking oil
2 teaspoons minced ginger
2 green onions, cut into 1-inch
　　pieces
⅓ cup diced carrots
1 rib celery, julienned
1 cup uncooked long-grain rice
1½ cups vegetable broth
¼ cup frozen peas, thawed
½ cup coarsely chopped toasted
　　walnuts

Method
1. Soak mushrooms in warm water to cover until softened, about 15 minutes; drain. Trim and discard stems. Thinly slice caps. Combine boiling water and tea leaves in a bowl; let steep for 15 minutes. Strain liquid tea into a bowl and discard tea leaves. Combine sauce ingredients in a bowl; set aside.

2. Place a 2-quart pot over high heat until hot. Add oil, swirling to coat sides. Add ginger and cook, stirring, until fragrant, about 10 seconds. Add mushrooms, green onions, carrots, and celery; stir-fry for 3 minutes. Add rice and mix well. Add liquid tea and broth; bring to a boil. Reduce heat to medium-high and cook, uncovered, until crater-like holes appear on rice.

3. Reduce heat to low, cover, and continue cooking until liquid is absorbed and rice is tender, 18 to 20 minutes.

4. Add peas and sauce; mix well. Remove to a serving bowl and garnish with walnuts.

Makes 4 to 6 servings

RICE FOR THE RUSHED

If you don't own an electric rice cooker, it's a modest investment that will be quickly repaid in convenience. It frees up space on the stove, and frees up your brain to worry about more important things. A 3-to-5-cup rice cooker is a good size for 1 to 4 people. Most rice cookers now have a "warmer" setting that keeps the rice hot once it's cooked. Microwave tip: Make extra rice and freeze it in heavy freezer bags. On busy nights, just zap and eat! (Before reheating, vent the bag by opening it slightly.)

Harvesting rice near Wuhan.

Wontons aren't just for appetizers and soups. Versatile wonton wrappers have a neutral flavor that goes perfectly with sweet ingredients, too. These crispy treats, filled with a chewy filling of dates, nuts and candied ginger, make a fun dessert. I sometimes serve them warm with a scoop of vanilla ice cream, but they're equally tasty at room temperature.

GINGER-DATE WONTONS

Filling
⅓ **cup chopped walnuts**
6 **Medjool dates, pitted and coarsely chopped**
3 **tablespoons chopped crystallized ginger**
1 **tablespoon grated lemon peel**
2 **teaspoons butter, softened**

24 **wonton wrappers**
Cooking oil for deep-frying

Method
1. Combine filling ingredients in a bowl; mix well.

2. To make each wonton, place 1 teaspoon filling in center of a wonton wrapper; keep remaining wrappers covered to prevent drying.

Brush edges of wrapper with water and fold wrapper in half to form a triangle. Pinch edges to seal. Pull two opposite corners together, moisten one corner, and overlap with the other corner; press to seal. Cover filled wonton with a dry towel to prevent drying.

3. Heat oil in a wok to 360°F over medium-high heat. Deep-fry wontons, half at a time, and cook, turning occasionally, until golden brown, 2 to 3 minutes. Remove and drain on paper towels. Serve hot or cold.

Makes 24

UP TO DATE

In China, dates date back centuries. The jujube, or Chinese red date, is small and wrinkled, with a sweet-tart flavor. In the U.S., it's sold only in dried form. The jujube bears no relation to the palm date—the kind familiar to Western cooks—or to the chewy candy of the same name! Palm dates came to China from Persia more than a thousand years ago. If you're looking for a great palm date, I recommend the large, moist, sweet Medjool, grown in California.

If you've ever tried steamed Chinese buns at a dim sum meal, you'll recognize the light yeast dough in these tender dessert dumplings. Here, I've used it to enclose a rich, sweet filling of dates and walnuts.

SWEET DATE BUNS

SHAPING SWEET DATE BUNS

Place filling in center of dough circle.

Gather dough around filling.

Steam buns, seam-side down, on paper.

1⅔ cups warm water (110°F)
1 package (¼ ounce) active dry
    yeast
5 cups all-purpose flour
¼ cup sugar

Filling
2 cups Medjool dates, pitted and
    mashed
⅓ cup finely chopped walnuts
¼ cup sugar
2 tablespoons ground toasted
    sesame seeds
¼ cup butter, softened

20 pieces parchment paper, each
    about 2-inches square

Method
1. Pour warm water into a bowl. Sprinkle yeast over water and stir until dissolved. Let stand until bubbles form, about 10 minutes. Combine filling ingredients in a bowl. Divide filling into 20 portions. Roll each portion into a ball; set aside.

2. Place flour and sugar in a food processor fitted with a metal blade; process for 10 seconds. With motor still running, pour

dissolved yeast down feed tube. Process until mixture forms a ball. Remove to a lightly floured board, knead dough until smooth and elastic, about 5 minutes. Place dough in a lightly greased bowl; turn to coat. Cover bowl with a dry towel. Let rise in a warm area until dough has doubled in bulk, about 1 hour.

3. Punch dough down. On a lightly floured board, roll dough into a cylinder then cut into 20 portions. To make each bun, roll a portion of dough into a 3½-inch to 4-inch circle, about ⅛-inch thick; keep remaining dough covered to prevent drying. Place a ball of filling in center of dough. Gather edges of dough around filling; pinch to seal.

4. Place a bun, seam side down, on a piece of parchment paper. Let buns rest for at least 5 minutes before steaming. Prepare a wok for steaming (see page 29). Cover and steam buns, half at a time, over high heat, 12 to 15 minutes.

Makes 20

In China, the word "tea" is sometimes used to describe sweet dessert soups like this one, which, in fact, contains no tea at all, and derives its refreshing sweetness from dates, rock sugar and crystallized ginger. Served in individual bowls, it's an exotic way to finish off a meal—and a sure-fire way to impress a "sweet date."

SWEET DATE TEA

3 cups water
¼ cup crushed rock sugar
⅓ cup diced crystallized ginger
2 tablespoons cornstarch dissolved
    in 3 tablespoons water
4 Medjool dates, pitted and thickly
    sliced
1 egg white, lightly beaten
4 quail eggs, poached, or hard-
    cooked and shelled
Mint sprigs for garnish

Method
1. Combine water, rock sugar, and crystallized ginger in a saucepan. Bring to a boil over medium heat. Reduce heat to low and cook, stirring, until rock sugar dissolves.

2. Increase heat to medium and add cornstarch solution; cook, stirring, until tea boils and thickens.

3. Add dates and cook for 1 minute. Turn off heat. Add egg white, stirring until it forms long threads.

4. Ladle into small bowls. Garnish each serving with a quail egg and a mint sprig.

Makes 4 servings

TEA FOR TWO

To the Chinese, tea is a symbol of friendship and fidelity, and there's a courtship ritual based on tea that dates back 1,500 years. First, a suitor would send a gift of tea to the family of his intended. If he was invited to her house, and met with the family's approval, he would be served three teas—one bitter, one sweet and gingery, and the third mellow and lingering. If the engagement were later broken, it was said in polite conversation that "the tea has been spilled."

At the teahouse in Shanghai's Wu Gardens, these charming *Bai* ladies served us afternoon tea.

Sichuan ~ The Spice

Westward ho! We're off to the region of Sichuan, the place I call the Wild West of China. The climate here is hot and humid, and the landscape is rugged, with rocky mountains, wide-open plains, deep gorges and mighty rivers. And that's reflected in the cuisine, which relies heavily on salt and assertive spices to liven up basic ingredients and preserved foods in the subtropical climate. Sichuanese cooking is famous

Box of China

for its explosive combinations of hot, sour, sweet and salty tastes, all in a single dish — drawing on seasonings like Sichuan peppercorns, star anise, vinegar, sugar, and, most notably, chiles — a trait shared by neighboring Hunan. Sesame seeds, peanuts, walnuts and cashews are popular here, and pickled, cured and smoked foods are a year-round mainstay.

These triangular "ravioli" in a spicy hot and sour broth were inspired by a dish we were served at the Chengdu Restaurant in Sichuan.

HOT AND SOUR DUMPLINGS IN CHILI BROTH

Filling
½ pound lean ground chicken
   or pork
3 tablespoons chicken broth
1 tablespoon oyster flavored sauce
2 teaspoons cornstarch

Broth
3 cups chicken broth
2 tablespoons black vinegar
2 tablespoons soy sauce
1 teaspoon chili sauce
1 teaspoon sugar

16 wonton wrappers
2 teaspoons cooking oil
2 cloves garlic, thinly sliced
2 teaspoons julienned ginger
½ cup thinly sliced carrots
8 snow peas, thinly sliced
1 jalapeño or serrano chili,
   thinly sliced

Method
1. Combine filling ingredients in a bowl; mix well. Let stand for 10 minutes. Combine chili broth ingredients in a bowl; set aside.

2. To fill each dumpling, place a heaping teaspoon of filling in center of a wonton wrapper; keep remaining wrappers covered to prevent drying. Brush edge of wrapper with water and fold wrapper in half to form a triangle. Pinch edges to seal. Cover filled dumplings with a dry towel.

3. Bring a pot of water to a boil. Add dumplings and cook until they float to the top, 2 to 3 minutes. Drain, rinse with cold water, and drain again.

4. Place a wok over high heat until hot. Add oil, swirling to coat sides. Add garlic and ginger; cook, stirring, until fragrant, about 10 seconds. Add carrots, snow peas, and chili; stir-fry until carrots are crisp-tender, 1 to 2 minutes. Add chili broth and bring to a boil.

5. Divide dumplings among 4 soup bowls. Ladle chili broth and vegetables over dumplings and serve.

Makes 4 servings

Of all Chinese soups, this one has become one of the great restaurant favorites all over the world. Don't be scared by the name—this version is only mildly hot, and has an extra aromatic kick from a non-traditional ingredient: lemongrass.

HOT AND SOUR SOUP WITH LEMONGRASS

4 dried black mushrooms
1 piece dried wood ear
¼ pound boneless, skinless chicken
    or lean pork
2 teaspoons cornstarch
½ package (7 ounces) regular-firm
    tofu, drained
5 cups chicken broth
1 stalk lemongrass (bottom 6 inches
    only), crushed or 1 tablespoon
    grated lemon peel
2 slices ginger, lightly crushed
½ cup julienned carrots
¼ cup julienned bamboo shoots
½ cup rice vinegar
3 tablespoons soy sauce
1 teaspoon chili sauce
3 tablespoons cornstarch dissolved
    in ¼ cup water
1 egg white, lightly beaten

Method

1. Soak mushrooms and wood ear in warm water to cover until softened, about 15 minutes; drain. Trim and discard stems. Thinly slice mushroom caps and wood ear.

2. Cut chicken into thin slices then cut slices into thin strips. Place in a bowl and add 2 teaspoons cornstarch; stir to coat. Let stand for 10 minutes. Cut tofu into ½-inch cubes.

3. Place broth in a 2-quart pot; bring to a boil. Add mushrooms, wood ear, lemongrass, and ginger. Reduce heat to low, cover, and simmer for 10 minutes. Discard lemongrass and ginger.

4. Add chicken, tofu, carrots, and bamboo shoots; cook for 2 minutes. Add vinegar, soy sauce, and chili sauce; bring to a boil.

5. Add cornstarch solution and cook, stirring, until soup boils and thickens. Turn off heat. Add egg white, stirring, until it forms long threads.

Makes 4 to 6 servings

LEMONGRASS

Lemongrass is commonly used in Thai and Vietnamese cooking, but I love to throw it into a few Chinese dishes every now and then. A slender, pale green stalk that looks a bit like a green onion, it gives foods a delicately fragrant citrus flavor. If you've ever bitten into a piece of lemongrass in a dish and thought you were chewing on a matchstick, you know that even after it's cooked it remains tough and woody. That's why it's often simmered in broths and sauces, then discarded before serving.

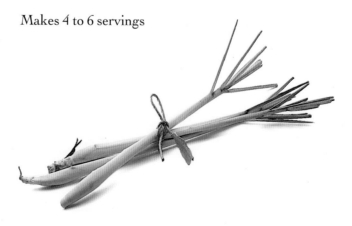

Sizzling Rice Soup always seems to inspire "oohs" and "ahs" when it's brought to the table in Chinese restaurants and the hot rice crusts are poured into the soup with a steaming, sizzling flourish. It's not hard to make this show-stopper at home.

SIZZLING RICE SOUP

½ pound boneless, skinless chicken

Marinade
1 tablespoon rice wine or dry sherry
1 teaspoon cornstarch

4 dried black mushrooms
6 cups chicken broth
¼ cup straw mushrooms
½ cup sliced bamboo shoots
½ cup sliced carrots
½ cup sliced zucchini
½ cup frozen peas, thawed
3 tablespoons rice wine
    or dry sherry
½ teaspoon salt
¼ teaspoon white pepper
Cooking oil for deep-frying
8 pieces rice crust, each
    about 2-inches square

Method
1. Cut chicken into thin slices then cut slices into thin strips. Combine marinade ingredients in a bowl. Add chicken and stir to coat. Let stand for 10 minutes.

2. Soak black mushrooms in warm water to cover until softened, about 15 minutes; drain. Trim and discard stems. Thinly slice caps.

3. Place broth in a large pot; bring to a boil. Add chicken, black mushrooms, and straw mushrooms. Reduce heat to low, cover, and simmer for 2 minutes. Add bamboo shoots, carrots, zucchini, peas, wine, salt, and pepper; simmer for about 2 minutes.

4. Heat oil in a wok to 375°F. Deep-fry rice crusts, one half at a time, and cook, turning continuously, until puffed and golden, 15 to 20 seconds. Remove and drain on paper towels.

5. To serve, bring soup to the table in a tureen. Slide hot rice crusts into hot soup and listen to the sizzle. Break rice crusts with ladle and serve.

Makes 6 to 8 servings

RICE CRUSTS
Rice crusts were originally a thrifty solution for using the toasted rice that remained caked at the bottom of a rice-cooking pot. Nowadays, you can buy square dried rice cakes in Asian markets. Or make your own: In a medium saucepan, bring 1 cup medium or short-grain rice and 1 cup water to a boil; reduce heat and simmer for 25 minutes. Let stand off-heat for 5 minutes. Spread rice in a ¼-inch-thick layer on a greased baking sheet. Cut rice into 2-inch squares with a wet knife. Bake at 325°F–350°F for 50 minutes until firm and dry.

Squid, shrimp and fish are first stir-fried, then quickly simmered in a flavorful broth. This Sichuanese-inspired double cooking method gives the seafood a more interesing texture and a deeper flavor than it would acquire from simply being simmered.

SEAFOOD MEDLEY IN CHILI BROTH

STOCK OPTIONS

Many recipes in this book call for chicken broth. Chinese soup stocks are simpler than Western ones. So it's easy to make your own: In a large pot, heat 8 cups water and 2½ pounds raw chicken bones to boiling. Skim off any foam that forms. Reduce heat, cover and simmer for 1½ hours. Add 4 halved green onions, 8 thin slices fresh ginger, and a pinch of salt and pepper. Simmer for 30 minutes. Strain broth, discarding bones and seasonings. If using canned broth, look for brands labeled "Oriental broth" or reduced-sodium broth.

2 small squid, cleaned
¼ pound medium raw shrimp, shelled and deveined
¼ pound firm white fish fillet, such as sea bass or red snapper

Marinade
2 teaspoons cornstarch
1 teaspoon salt

4 cups chicken broth
½ cup sliced carrots
2 tablespoons julienned ginger
2 tablespoons cooking oil
6 small dried red chiles
¼ cup rice wine or dry sherry
1 tablespoon soy sauce
1 teaspoon sesame oil
2 tablespoons cornstarch dissolved in 3 tablespoons water
1 egg white, lightly beaten

Method
1. Cut squid, shrimp, and fish into ¾-inch pieces. Combine marinade ingredients in a bowl. Add seafood and stir to coat. Let stand for 10 minutes.

2. Place broth, carrots, and ginger in a 2-quart pot; bring to a boil. Reduce heat to low and simmer for 2 minutes.

3. Place a wok over high heat until hot. Add cooking oil, swirling to coat sides. Add chiles and cook, stirring, until fragrant, about 10 seconds. Add seafood and stir-fry for 1 minute.

4. Pour seafood into broth and simmer for 1 minute. Add wine, soy sauce, and sesame oil. Add cornstarch solution and cook, stirring, until soup boils and thickens. Turn off heat. Add egg white, stirring, until it forms long threads.

Makes 4 servings

This hearty, home-style soup is made with flavorful beef shank meat, slowly simmered to bring out its rich taste. It's quick to put together, but the simmering takes a while, so make it when you have a few hours to relax and enjoy the fragrance of star anise and ginger that will fill your kitchen.

FRAGRANT BEEF SOUP

¾ **pound boneless beef shank**

Marinade
2 tablespoons dark soy sauce
2 teaspoons cornstarch

2 ribs celery
1 carrot
½ pound daikon
2 tablespoons cooking oil
4 cups beef broth
1 cup water
4 slices ginger, lightly crushed
2 whole star anise
1 tablespoon regular soy sauce
2 teaspoons sugar
¼ teaspoon white pepper

Method
1. Cut beef into ½-inch pieces. Combine marinade ingredients in a bowl. Add beef and stir to coat. Let stand for 10 minutes. Thinly slice celery. Roll cut carrot and daikon.

2. Place a wide frying pan over high heat until hot. Add oil, swirling to coat sides. Add beef and cook until browned on all sides, 2 to 3 minutes.

3. Lift beef from pan drippings and place in a 2-quart pot. Add broth, water, ginger, and star anise; bring to a boil. Reduce heat to low, cover, and simmer until meat is tender, 45 to 50 minutes.

4. Add celery, carrot, and daikon. Cover and simmer until vegetables are tender, 15 to 20 minutes. Add soy sauce, sugar, and pepper; simmer for 5 minutes.

Makes 4 to 6 servings

ON DAIKON

Daikon is the Japanese name for a long white radish that looks like an over-sized carrot. It's also known as the Chinese turnip or Chinese radish. Raw daikon has a delicious, sweet, mildly peppery flavor. It's used in Japanese cooking in a variety of ways—in salads, shaved into thin threads as an accompaniment to sashimi, and fried as tempura. In China, it's most often used in slow-cooked stews, soups and braised dishes, much like the western turnip or potato.

163

This unusual Sichuanese-style salad of julienned chicken, ham, carrot and cucumber is colorful and refreshing, with a wonderful combination of chewy and crunchy textures. Try the tangy sesame dressing with salad greens or noodles, too.

SILK THREAD CHICKEN SALAD

AGAR AGAR

You remember it from your biology class, but perhaps you'll be surprised to learn that agar agar is a common ingredient in Chinese cooking. Made from seaweed, it's Asia's answer to gelatin. It's sold in Asian markets as a powder, in sheets, or in strips. Agar agar can be used like gelatin to set desserts and cold salads. The strips, which look like foot-long crumpled strands of cellophane tape are often soaked in warm water and used in tossed cold salads to add a delightful crunchy texture.

1 ounce dried agar agar strips, cut into 2-inch lengths

Dressing
3 tablespoons rice vinegar
3 tablespoons sesame seed paste or chunky peanut butter
2 tablespoons honey
1 tablespoon sesame oil
1 teaspoon soy sauce
1 teaspoon dried mustard
½ teaspoon salt
1 teaspoon finely chopped cilantro

⅓ cup shredded cooked chicken breast
⅓ cup julienned ham
½ cup julienned carrots
½ cucumber, julienned

Method
1. Soak agar agar in warm water to cover until softened, about 15 minutes; drain. Parboil agar agar in a pot of boiling water for 10 seconds. Drain, rinse with cold water, and drain again.

2. Prepare dressing: Combine vinegar and sesame seed paste in a bowl; whisk until blended. Add remaining dressing ingredients and mix well.

3. Place agar agar in a salad bowl. Add dressing, chicken, ham, carrots, and cucumber; toss to coat.

Makes 4 to 6 servings

Sichuan is famous for its cold noodle dishes, which are often tossed in a spicy sesame or peanut dressing like this one. You can use any kind of cooked chicken breast meat in this salad—roasted, poached, pan-fried or grilled—but it's particularly delicious with White-Cut Chicken (page 109).

COLD MIXED NOODLES, SICHUAN-STYLE

1 package (about 12 ounces) fresh
   Chinese egg or spinach noodles
2 teaspoons sesame oil
½ cucumber, julienned
½ red bell pepper, julienned
¼ pound fresh mung bean sprouts
2 cups shredded cooked chicken
   breast

Dressing
⅓ cup chicken broth
⅓ cup sesame seed paste or chunky
   peanut butter
2 tablespoons soy sauce
2 tablespoons rice vinegar
2 teaspoons sesame oil
2 teaspoons chili sauce
½ teaspoon sugar
½ teaspoon ground toasted Sichuan
   peppercorns

Method
1. Cook noodles in a pot of boiling water according to package directions. Drain, rinse with cold water, and drain again. Place noodles in a bowl and add sesame oil; toss to coat.

2. Add cucumber, bell pepper, and mung bean sprouts; toss to mix. Place on a serving plate and arrange chicken over the top. Cover and refrigerate until chilled.

3. Prepare dressing: Combine broth and sesame seed paste in a bowl; whisk until blended. Add remaining dressing ingredients and mix well.

4. Pour dressing over noodles and toss before serving.

Makes 4 to 6 servings

PEANUT GALLERY
When is a nut not a nut? When it's a peanut! It's actually a legume, like the soybean, the lentil or the pea (which explains how it got its name in the first place). By Chinese standards, peanuts are a relatively "new" ingredient, having arrived from the New World a mere 400 years ago. But in that time, they've become China's most important source of cooking oil and—being rich in protein —a dietary staple. They're eaten as a snack, added to stir-fries and sweets, and ground for use in dressings, sauces and soups.

When the weather warms up and asparagus is in season, I like to prepare it Sichuanese-style: quickly blanched in boiling water until crisp-tender, then chilled and tossed in a sweet, mustardy dressing. This dish is easy to prepare ahead of time, but wait until the last minute to add the dressing so the asparagus retains its bright green color.

ASPARAGUS WITH SWEET AND PUNGENT DRESSING

MUSTARD'S A MUST

Dried mustard gives foods a mysterious, pleasantly hot flavor, especially when you use it in moderation, adding just a pinch to sauces and dressings. In China, prepared mustard is often served as a condiment with appetizers and cold platters. To make your own, pour some powdered Chinese or English mustard into a bowl and whisk in drops of water until you get the consistency you want. If you let it stand for an hour or more, you'll find that the flavor develops and the bitterness disappears.

1 pound asparagus, trimmed
1 teaspoon cooking oil
½ teaspoon salt

Dressing
2 tablespoons plum sauce
2 tablespoons rice vinegar
2 tablespoons soy sauce
1 tablespoon sesame oil
1 teaspoon chili oil
2 teaspoons sugar or honey
½ teaspoon dried mustard

**Chopped toasted walnuts
    for garnish**

Method
1. Cut asparagus diagonally into 1½-inch slices. Bring a pot of water to a boil. Add oil, salt, and asparagus. Cook until asparagus is crisp-tender, 1 to 2 minutes. Drain, rinse with cold water, and drain again. Pat dry with paper towels.

2. Combine dressing ingredients in a bowl. Add asparagus and toss to coat.

3. Arrange asparagus on a serving plate and garnish with walnuts.

Makes 4 servings

The creamy texture of bean curd and the crunch of walnuts, water chestnuts and carrots make a delightful yin-and-yang combination in this vegetarian stir-fry —all brought together in a sweet and spicy sauce.

BRAISED BEAN CURD WITH WALNUTS

WATER CHESTNUTS

Canned water chestnuts are widely available. Fresh ones are a little harder to find, but worth searching for (look in Asian groceries when they're in season). Their meat is sweeter and their texture crisper than their canned counterparts. Don't be put off by fresh water chestnuts' muddy exterior. Rinse them well, then peel the brown skin with a paring knife, placing the peeled ones in water as you work to prevent discoloration. Fresh jícama can be used as a substitute for water chestnuts.

½ cup frozen baby lima beans, thawed
1 package (14 ounces) regular-firm or extra-firm tofu (bean curd), drained

Sauce
½ cup vegetable broth
1 tablespoon regular soy sauce
1 tablespoon dark soy sauce
1 teaspoon chili garlic sauce
1 teaspoon sesame oil
1 teaspoon sugar

1½ tablespoons cooking oil
6 small dried red chiles
4 large white button mushrooms, sliced
½ cup straw mushrooms
1 can (5 ounces) whole water chestnuts, drained and diced
¼ cup diced carrots
1 ½ teaspoons cornstarch dissolved in 1 tablespoon water
¾ cup toasted walnut halves

Method
1. Parboil lima beans in a pot of boiling water for 3 minutes; drain. Cut tofu into ½-inch cubes. Combine sauce ingredients in a bowl; set aside.

2. Place a wok over high heat until hot. Add oil, swirling to coat sides. Add chiles and cook, stirring, until fragrant, about 10 seconds. Add lima beans, tofu, all mushrooms, water chestnuts, and carrots; stir-fry until carrots are crisp-tender, about 1½ minutes.

3. Add sauce and bring to a boil. Add cornstarch solution and cook, stirring, until sauce boils and thickens. Add walnuts and toss to coat.

Makes 4 to 6 servings

This is my version of the famous Sichuanese dish, Ma Po Bean Curd—silky tofu in a spicy meat sauce that has the wonderful, smoky-spicy flavor of toasted Sichuan peppercorns.

FRAGRANT PEPPERCORN TOFU

Marinade
1 tablespoon oyster flavored sauce
1 teaspoon cornstarch

½ pound lean ground chicken, pork, or beef
1 package (14 ounces) regular-firm tofu, drained

Sauce
⅓ cup chicken broth
2 tablespoons soy sauce
1½ teaspoons chili garlic sauce
1 teaspoon black bean garlic sauce
1 teaspoon cornstarch
1 teaspoon sugar
½ teaspoon ground toasted Sichuan peppercorns

2 tablespoons cooking oil
2 tablespoons minced garlic
Chopped green onions for garnish

Method
1. Combine marinade ingredients in a bowl. Add chicken and mix well. Let stand for 10 minutes. Cut tofu into ½-inch cubes. Combine sauce ingredients in a bowl; set aside.

2. Place a wok over high heat until hot. Add oil, swirling to coat sides. Add garlic and cook, stirring, until fragrant, about 10 seconds. Add meat and stir-fry for 2 minutes. Add tofu and sauce. Cook, stirring gently, until tofu is heated through and sauce boils and thickens. Place in a serving bowl and garnish with green onions.

Makes 4 servings

SICHUAN PEPPERCORNS
No relation to black peppercorns, Sichuan peppercorns are actually a dried berry that's used as a seasoning throughout western China. Along with star anise, they're one of the main ingredients in Chinese five-spice powder. When Sichuan peppercorns are toasted, their fragrant oils are released, and they take on a pleasant spiciness that's less sharp than black pepper or chiles. Toast them in a dry, heavy frying pan over low heat, stirring occasionally, until they become fragrant.

In rural Sichuan, when it comes to harvesting and drying Sichuan peppercorns, everybody gets into the act.

169

This cold salad made with slippery, translucent bean thread noodles and julienned vegetables in a sesame vinaigrette dressing, makes a perfect dish for a picnic or a light meal at home. See how much fun noodles can be?

SPICY FUN SEE NOODLE SALAD

8 ounces dried bean thread noodles
   (fun see)

Dressing
2 tablespoons soy sauce
2 tablespoons rice vinegar
1 tablespoon oyster flavored sauce
2 teaspoons chili garlic sauce
2 teaspoons sesame oil
1 teaspoon sugar

1 teaspoon sesame oil
2 green onions, julienned
1 carrot, julienned
½ cucumber, julienned

Method

1. Soak bean thread noodles in warm water to cover until softened, about 15 minutes; drain. Cut bean thread noodles into 4-inch lengths. Combine dressing ingredients in a bowl; set aside.

2. Bring a pot of water to a boil. Add bean thread noodles and cook for 1 minute. Drain, rinse with cold water, and drain again. Pat dry with paper towels.

3. Place bean thread noodles in a salad bowl and toss with sesame oil. Add dressing, green onions, carrot, and cucumber; toss to coat.

Makes 4 to 6 servings

FUN

Fun is the Chinese word for rice noodles. But it's also the English word for having a good time! I think having fun in the kitchen and "playing with your food" is one of the most rewarding parts of cooking. When you try new ingredients and recipes with a sense of adventure, you're doing more than just putting food on the table. You're sharing the excitement of creating something new. Serve your creation with a smile and you add a little happiness to the world. And that, after all, is what fun is all about.

Here's my take on a traditional Sichuanese banquet dish we were served at the Chengdu Restaurant in Chengdu, Sichuan—shredded chicken and vegetables tossed in a warm sauce that heats the ingredients just enough to take away their raw edge. Use White-Cut Chicken (page 109) or leftover poached or roasted chicken.

WARM CHICKEN SALAD

1 ½ cups shredded cooked chicken breast
1 cup julienned carrots
½ cup julienned cucumbers
1 green onion, julienned
1 red bell pepper, julienned

Sauce
⅓ cup rice vinegar
2 tablespoons soy sauce
1 tablespoon sesame oil
2 teaspoons chili garlic sauce
1 teaspoon chili oil
4 teaspoons sugar

2 teaspoons cooking oil
1 tablespoon minced garlic
1 teaspoon cornstarch dissolved in 2 teaspoons water
Toasted sesame seeds and toasted walnut halves for garnish

Method
1. Combine chicken, carrots, cucumbers, green onion, and bell pepper in a bowl. Combine sauce ingredients in another bowl; set aside.

2. Place a wok over high heat until hot. Add oil, swirling to coat sides. Add garlic and cook, stirring, until fragrant, about 10 seconds. Add sauce and bring to a boil. Add cornstarch solution and cook, stirring, until sauce boils and thickens. Let cool slightly.

3. Pour warm sauce over chicken mixture and toss to coat. Arrange on a serving plate and garnish with sesame seeds and walnuts.

Fresh mung bean sprouts can be eaten raw, but they taste even better when you quickly parboil them, then chill them for use in salads like this one. Here, they're paired with soft tofu and drizzled with a sweet and spicy dressing.

CHILLED TOFU WITH BEAN SPROUTS

½ pound fresh mung bean sprouts

Dressing
3 tablespoons rice vinegar
2 tablespoons soy sauce
2 tablespoons sesame oil
1 tablespoon chili garlic sauce
2 teaspoons sugar or honey

1 package (16 ounces) soft tofu, drained
1 teaspoon toasted white sesame seeds
½ teaspoon black sesame seeds
¼ cup chopped toasted walnuts

Method
1. Parboil mung bean sprouts in a pot of boiling water for 1 minute. Drain, rinse with cold water, and drain again. Remove to a serving plate, cover, and refrigerate until chilled.

2. Combine dressing ingredients in a bowl; set aside.

3. Cut tofu into ½-inch cubes. Place over chilled mung bean sprouts. Drizzle dressing over tofu and garnish with sesame seeds and walnuts.

Makes 4 servings

MUNG BEAN MAGIC

Growing your own fresh mung bean sprouts is easy and surprisingly fast. Wash ½ cup of dried green mung beans and place them in a 1-quart jar with 2 cups of cold water. Cover the jar with cheesecloth, secured with a rubber band. The next day, drain the water, rinse the beans, drain again and let stand overnight. Repeat for 1 or 2 more days, until the familiar long white sprouts appear and reach 2 to 3 inches in length. Pick off the green husks, rinse the sprouts, and they're ready to eat.

Two of Sichuan's most popular ingredients—tender bamboo shoots and mushrooms—come together in this tasty stir-fry. If you can find Sichuan preserved vegetables, give them a try. Cured in brine with chiles and Sichuan peppercorns, they add an intriguing, spicy, pickled flavor, a bit like Korean kimchee.

BRAISED BAMBOO SHOOTS WITH TWO MUSHROOMS

THE BEAUTY OF BAMBOO

With its hot, tropical climate, Sichuan is the "bamboo bayou" of China. Bamboo is actually not a tree, but a giant grass that grows to heights of up to 100 feet. In China, it's used in construction, for making all kinds of utensils and furniture and even for paper-making and fuel. The tender bamboo shoot, sold in cans in the U.S., has a sweet flavor and a delicately crunchy texture. To refresh canned bamboo shoots, blanch them for a few seconds in boiling water before using them in cooking.

A bamboo forest in Sichuan.

14 small dried black mushrooms
8 ounces whole bamboo shoots

Sauce
½ chicken broth
¼ cup water
2 tablespoons oyster flavored sauce
2 tablespoons soy sauce
1 teaspoon chili garlic sauce
1½ teaspoons packed brown sugar

½ pound small white mushrooms
1 tablespoon cooking oil
2 cloves garlic, lightly crushed
2 slices ginger, lightly crushed
2 tablespoons chopped Sichuan preserved vegetable (optional)
¼ pound snow peas, trimmed
1½ teaspoons cornstarch dissolved in 1 tablespoon water

Method

1. Soak black mushrooms in warm water to cover until softened, about 15 minutes; drain. Trim and discard stems. Leave caps whole. Roll cut bamboo shoots. Combine sauce ingredients in a bowl; set aside.

2. Parboil bamboo shoots and button mushrooms in boiling water for 1 minute; drain.

3. Place a 2-quart pot over high heat until hot. Add oil, swirling to coat sides. Add garlic and ginger; cook, stirring, until fragrant, about 10 seconds. Add black mushrooms, bamboo shoots, button mushrooms, and preserved vegetable; stir-fry for 30 seconds. Add sauce and bring to a boil.

4. Reduce heat to low, cover, and simmer for 10 minutes. Add snow peas and cook until crisp-tender, about 1 minute. Add cornstarch solution and cook, stirring until sauce boils and thickens.

Makes 4 servings

*T*alk about singing for your supper! In this dramatic banquet-style dish, a flavorful stir-fry of seafood and vegetables is poured over sizzling rice crusts (see note, page 161) for a show-stopping tableside presentation.

SEAFOOD OVER SINGING RICE

Marinade
2 teaspoons cornstarch
½ teaspoon salt

¼ pound sea scallops, cut in
    half horizontally
¼ pound medium raw shrimp,
    shelled and deveined

Sauce
⅓ cup chicken broth
⅓ cup sweet chili sauce
2 teaspoons soy sauce
1 teaspoon sesame oil
2 teaspoons cornstarch

2 tablespoons cooking oil
1 can (5 ounces) sliced bamboo
    shoots, drained
½ cup straw mushrooms
½ cup sliced carrots
¼ pound snow peas, trimmed and
    cut in half
Cooking oil for deep-frying
12 pieces rice crust, each
    about 2 inches square

Method
1. Combine marinade ingredients in a bowl. Add scallops and shrimp; stir to coat. Let stand for 10 minutes. Combine sauce ingredients in a bowl; set aside.

2. Place a wok over high heat until hot. Add 2 tablespoons oil, swirling to coat sides. Add scallops and shrimp; stir-fry for 1 minute. Add bamboo shoots, straw mushrooms, carrots, and snow peas; stir-fry until carrots and snow peas are crisp-tender, about 2 minutes. Add sauce and cook until heated through. Remove from heat, cover, and keep warm while you deep-fry rice crusts.

3. Heat oil in a wok to 375°F. Deep-fry rice crusts, one half at a time, and cook, turning continuously, until puffed and golden, 15 to 20 seconds. Remove and drain on paper towels.

4. Place hot rice crusts on a serving plate and immediately pour hot seafood mixture over the top.

Makes 4 servings

SCALLOPS
Two types of scallops are most commonly sold in the U.S.: sea scallops and bay scallops. Larger sea scallops have a nice chewy texture, that's great for stir-fries. You can cut them in half horizontally so that they cook more evenly. Bay scallops are smaller and sweeter and have a more delicate texture. In fine restaurants in China, scallops are more likely to be used dried than fresh. A prized delicacy along the lines of shark's fin, dried scallops are used as a flavoring in soups and sauces.

I think there's no better way to enjoy fresh fish than this classic Chinese method—steaming it whole with aromatic vegetables and dressing it with hot oil and a simple sauce.

STEAMED FISH WITH SIZZLING LEMONGRASS OIL

5 dried black mushrooms
2 stalks lemongrass (bottom 6 inches
    only)
4 green onions

Sizzling Oil
3 tablespoons cooking oil
2 teaspoons sesame oil
1 stalk lemongrass (bottom 6 inches
    only), thinly sliced

Fish Dressing
¼ cup soy sauce
3 tablespoons chicken broth
1 tablespoon oyster flavored sauce
2 teaspoons sugar

1 whole fish (1½ to 2 pounds),
    such as sea bass or red snapper,
    cleaned and scaled
½ teaspoon salt
½ teaspoon white pepper
10 slices ginger, lightly crushed

Method
1. Soak mushrooms in warm water
to cover until softened, about 15
minutes; drain. Trim and discard
stems. Halve caps. Cut each piece
of lemongrass into 5 slanting slices.
Julienne 2 green onions and leave
remaining 2 green onions whole.

Combine sizzling lemongrass oil
ingredients in a saucepan; set aside.
Combine fish dressing ingredients
in another saucepan; set aside.

2. Cut fish ¾-inch deep along verte-
brae on each side of bone. Cut 5 slits
lengthwise, ¾-inch deep, on both sides
of fish as illustrated. Sprinkle fish
with salt and pepper. Place a piece of
mushroom, lemongrass, and ginger
in each slit.

3. Place whole green onions in center
of a heat-proof glass pie dish; lay fish
on top. Prepare a wok for steaming
(see page 29). Cover and steam fish
over high heat until fish turns
opaque, 8 to 10 minutes.

4. Sprinkle half the julienned
green onion over fish. Heat sizzling
lemongrass oil over high heat until
hot; drizzle over fish. Heat fish
dressing over high heat and cook
until heated through; pour over fish.
Garnish with remaining julienned
green onions.

Makes 4 to 6 servings

THE WHOLE FISH

What makes whole fish so
popular in China? First, the
bones, the head, the gills
and the fins all add a lot of
flavor to the fish as it cooks.
Then there's the symbolic
value. A whole fish is a regular fixture at special meals
because it symbolizes abundance and fullness. It's such
an important symbol that in
land-locked regions where
fish is unavailable, a stand-in
wooden fish is sometimes
presented! When serving a
whole fish, it's customary in
China to point the head
toward the guest of honor.

Wok-smoking over rice and tea is a common food preservation technique in hot, humid Sichuan. It's also a wonderful way to flavor foods, no matter where in the world you live.

WOK-SMOKED FISH

1 ½ pounds firm white fish fillets, such as sea bass or red snapper, about ½-inch thick

Marinade
2 teaspoons minced ginger
¼ cup rice wine or dry sherry
3 tablespoons regular soy sauce
3 tablespoons dark soy sauce
½ teaspoon liquid smoke (optional)
2 teaspoons sugar
½ teaspoon Chinese five-spice
½ teaspoon ground toasted Sichuan peppercorns

Smoking Mixture
½ cup packed brown sugar
⅓ cup uncooked long-grain rice
⅓ cup black or oolong tea leaves

Julienned honeydew melon and cantaloupe for garnish

Method
1. Cut fish crosswise to make 3-inch square pieces. Combine marinade ingredients in a bowl. Add fish and stir to coat. Let stand for 10 minutes.

2. Combine smoking mixture ingredients and spread evenly in a foil-lined wok. Set a round cake rack over smoking mixture. Place fish on rack and place wok over high heat.

3. When mixture begins to smoke, cover wok with a foil-lined lid; reduce heat to medium-low and smoke until fish flakes with a fork, 7 or 8 minutes.

4. Turn off heat and allow to sit with lid on for 5 minutes. Serve fish hot or cold, garnished with melon.

Makes 4 servings

This dish is designed for sharing—perfect for a romantic dinner for two. It's stir-fried prawns presented two ways: half served in a tangy tomato sauce, the other half in a spicy curry sauce.

THE TRUE LOVER'S PRAWNS

Marinade
2 teaspoons cornstarch
½ teaspoon salt

1 ½ pounds medium raw prawns,
    shelled and deveined

Sauce A
3 tablespoons ketchup
1 tablespoon plum sauce
½ teaspoon chili paste
1 teaspoon sugar

Sauce B
2 tablespoons prepared curry sauce
2 tablespoons rice wine
    or dry sherry

2 small tomatoes, cut in half and
    thinly sliced
1 ½ tablespoons cooking oil
1 teaspoon minced garlic
1 teaspoon minced lemon peel

Method
1. Combine marinade ingredients in a bowl. Add prawns and stir to coat. Let stand for 10 minutes. Combine sauce A in a bowl; set aside. Combine sauce B in another bowl; set aside.

2. Arrange tomato slices in center of a serving plate to form a tomato "wall".

3. Place a wok over high heat until hot. Add oil, swirling to coat sides. Add garlic, and lemon peel; cook, stirring, until fragrant, about 10 seconds. Add prawns and stir-fry until prawns turn pink, 2½ to 3 minutes. Remove half the prawns to a bowl; set aside.

4. Add sauce A to prawns in wok; stir-fry for 30 seconds. Remove prawns and arrange on one side of the serving plate. Wipe wok with a damp towel. Return remaining prawns to wok. Add sauce B and stir-fry for 30 seconds. Arrange on other side of the serving plate.

Makes 4 servings

CHEERS!

In China, there's a whole code of etiquette surrounding the serving of wine and tea. If you're pouring wine for a guest, always fill the glass to the brim as a sign of respect. With tea, it's a different story: filling the cup more than half-way is a sign of disrespect. When it comes to toasting, show respect by clinking your glass below your guest's. If you get confused, just remember my first rule of dining etiquette: "be nice, and always offer to pick up the tab."

Curry in a hurry: You can toss this simple seafood stir-fry with a light curry sauce together in just a few minutes, especially if you start with shelled, deveined shrimp.

CURRIED SHRIMP AND SCALLOPS

LETTER FROM LESHAN

"I'm standing at the feet of the most awe-inspiring statue I have ever seen: Dafo, the Grand Buddha, carved into the rock face at Leshan, Sichuan, 1,300 years ago. It's the largest Buddha in the world—the height of a twenty-story building—an astonishing feat of engineering. The proportions are staggering: Dafo's big toe is 27 feet long! What must it have been like to create a monument like this so many centuries ago? And what sweeping changes has Dafo witnessed as he gazes across the river in silent contemplation?"

Marinade
1 teaspoon cornstarch
¼ teaspoon salt

½ pound medium raw shrimp, shelled and deveined
½ pound sea scallops, cut in half horizontally

Sauce
¼ cup prepared curry sauce
¼ cup rice wine or dry sherry
2 teaspoons soy sauce

2½ tablespoons cooking oil
1 teaspoon minced ginger
½ onion, cut into 1-inch pieces
½ each red and green bell pepper, cut into 1-inch squares

Method
1. Combine marinade ingredients in a bowl. Add shrimp and scallops; stir to coat. Let stand for 10 minutes. Combine sauce ingredients in a bowl; set aside.

2. Place a wok over high heat until hot. Add 2 tablespoons oil, swirling to coat sides. Add shrimp and scallops; stir-fry for 1 minute. Remove shrimp and scallops from wok.

3. Add remaining ½ tablespoon oil to wok, swirling to coat sides. Add ginger and onion; stir-fry for 30 seconds. Add bell peppers and stir-fry for 1 minute. Return shrimp and scallops to wok and add sauce; cook until heated through.

Makes 4 servings

What makes this chicken so special? It's cooked by three methods: it's quickly browned in oil for color and flavor, cooked with moist heat in a steamer, and finally wok-smoked over tea and rice to give it a distinctive smoky flavor.

TEA-SMOKED CHICKEN

4 chicken thighs or 6 drumsticks

Marinade
2 tablespoons dark soy sauce
2 tablespoons rice wine
   or dry sherry
2 teaspoons cornstarch

2 tablespoons cooking oil

Smoking Mixture
½ cup packed brown sugar
⅓ cup uncooked long-grain rice
¼ cup black or oolong tea leaves
4 slices ginger, lightly crushed
2 whole star anise
2 teaspoons liquid smoke
   or ¼ cup hickory chips

Method
1. If using chicken thighs, place chicken, skin side down, on a cutting board. With a sharp knife, cut slits ½-inch deep along both sides of the bone. Combine marinade ingredients in a bowl. Add chicken and stir to coat. Let stand for 10 minutes.

2. Place a wide frying pan over medium heat until hot. Add oil, swirling to coat sides. Add chicken and cook until golden brown on all sides, 2 to 3 minutes per side.

3. Prepare a wok for steaming (see page 29). Cover and steam chicken over high heat for 30 minutes.

4. Combine smoking mixture and spread evenly in a foil-lined wok. Set a round cake rack over smoking mixture. Place chicken, breast side up, on rack and place wok over high heat. When mixture begins to smoke, cover wok with a foil-lined lid; reduce heat to medium-low and smoke until chicken takes a rich deep color, 12 to 15 minutes. Turn off heat and allow to sit with lid on for 5 minutes. Serve chicken hot or at room temperature.

Makes 4 servings

TEA

Tea is native to China, and it was the Chinese who first discovered that a flavorful infusion could be made by boiling the leaves of tea shrubs in water about 4,000 years ago. From China, tea found its way to Japan in the 8th century, A.D., and eventually to Europe in the 17th century. The humble cup of tea is one of China's greatest gifts to the world. To me, it's more than a beverage. It's a chance to escape from the hubbub of life, relax, and enjoy a quite moment of reflection.

Drying green tea the old-fashioned way, in the cast-iron bowl of a drying stove.

This recipe is based on a method used in the province of Yunnan, to the south of Sichuan. Chicken or game hen is first parboiled to remove some fat, then placed in a pot of aromatic broth, which is, in turn, placed inside a steamer and slowly simmered. This gentle cooking method produces succulent, tender chicken and a rich, complex broth.

DOUBLE-STEAMED CHICKEN

4 dried black mushrooms
2 pieces dried wood ear (optional)
1 small Rock Cornish game hen,
　　cleaned or 1 pound boneless,
　　skinless chicken
6 dried jujubes (optional)
4 Medjool dates, pitted
4 slices ginger, lightly crushed
2 tablespoons chopped ham
¼ cup walnut halves
　　or raw skinless peanuts
3 cups chicken broth
¾ cup Shao Hsing wine
1 teaspoon salt

Method

1. Soak mushrooms and wood ears in warm water to cover until softened, about 15 minutes; drain. Trim and discard stems. Halve mushroom caps and cut wood ears into bite-size pieces.

2. Place game hen in a pot and cover with water; bring to a boil. Parboil for 1 minute; drain. Place game hen in a 2-quart casserole and add remaining ingredients; cover.

3. Prepare a wok for steaming (see page 29). Place covered casserole on steaming rack. Cover wok and steam over boiling water until game hen is tender, 1½ to 2 hours. Add water to steamer as needed.

Makes 6 servings

THE YUNNAN POT

To prepare this recipe, you can use any casserole that will fit inside your steamer, but if you can find an authentic Yunnan pot, so much the better. Sold in Chinese specialty shops, it's a round pot made of red clay with a chimney that comes half-way up its center, stopping just below the lid. Food is placed around the chimney, and the pot is covered and placed inside a steamer. The steam comes up through the chimney into the pot and slowly cooks the food, making it moist and succulent.

Double-Steamed Chicken in a Yunnan pot

Here's my recipe for one of the most famous of all Sichuan/Hunanese dishes—hot, sour, sweet and savory Kung Pao Chicken. To make it even hotter, break open one or more of the dried chili pods before adding them to the wok.

KUNG PAO CHICKEN

CHILI TODAY

Chiles are popular in Sichuan and Hunan because they grow in abundance and because eating them induces sweating and cools the body, providing relief from the heat. There are more than 200 kinds of chiles, from foot-long giants to pea-sized miniatures. How much heat they give a dish depends on the type you use, whether it's fresh, dried, whole or crushed, and how you prepare it. If you're feeling timid, start by removing the seeds and membrane, since that's where most of the heat is.

¾ pound boneless, skinless chicken

Marinade
2 tablespoons oyster flavored sauce
1 teaspoon cornstarch

Sauce
¼ cup black vinegar or balsamic
    vinegar
¼ cup chicken broth
3 tablespoons rice wine
    or dry sherry
2 tablespoons hoisin sauce
1 tablespoon soy sauce
2 teaspoons sesame oil
2 teaspoons chili garlic sauce
2 teaspoons sugar

2½ tablespoons cooking oil
8 small dried red chiles
4 teaspoons minced garlic
2 ribs celery, diced
½ red bell pepper, cut into 1-inch-
    squares

½ cup diced bamboo shoots
2 teaspoons cornstarch dissolved in
    1 tablespoon water
½ cup toasted walnut halves

Method
1. Cut chicken into 1-inch pieces. Combine marinade ingredients in a bowl. Add chicken and stir to coat. Let stand for 10 minutes. Combine sauce ingredients in a bowl; set aside.

2. Place a wok over high heat until hot. Add 2 tablespoons oil, swirling to coat sides. Add chiles and cook, stirring, until fragrant, about 10 seconds. Add chicken and stir-fry for 2 minutes. Remove the chicken and chiles from the wok.

3. Add remaining ½ tablespoon oil, swirling to coat sides. Add garlic and cook, stirring, until fragrant, about 10 seconds. Add celery, bell pepper, and bamboo shoots; stir-fry for 1½ minutes. Return chicken and chiles to wok; stir-fry for 1 minute. Add sauce and bring to a boil. Add cornstarch solution and cook, stirring, until sauce boils and thickens. Add walnuts and toss to coat.

Makes 4 servings

Shopping for chiles at an open-air market.

Dry-frying is a typical western Chinese cooking method in which vegetables are first deep fried, then stir-fried, giving them a chewy texture. Here's an easier method—the beans are quickly parboiled in water before stir-frying. Chinese yard-long beans, cut into 3-inch lengths are also wonderful in this recipe.

HUNAN BEEF WITH DRY-FRIED BEANS

Marinade
1 tablespoon soy sauce
1 tablespoon cornstarch

¾ pound flank steak,
    cut into ½-inch cubes

Sauce
¼ cup chicken broth
¼ cup rice wine or dry sherry
2 tablespoons soy sauce
1 tablespoon black bean sauce
2 teaspoons chili garlic sauce
2 teaspoons sesame oil
1 teaspoon minced jalapeño
    or serrano chili
1 tablespoon sugar
1½ teaspoons cornstarch

3 tablespoons cooking oil
¾ pound green beans, trimmed and
    cut into 2-inch pieces
6 small dried red chiles
1 tablespoon minced garlic

Method
1. Combine marinade ingredients in a bowl. Add beef and stir to coat. Let stand for 10 minutes. Combine sauce ingredients in a bowl; set aside.

2. Parboil green beans in a pot of boiling water for 3 minutes; drain.

3. Place a wok over high heat until hot. Add oil, swirling to coat sides. Add green beans; stir-fry until green beans are slightly wilted, 3 to 4 minutes. Remove the beans from the wok.

4. Remove all but 1½ tablespoons oil from wok. Add chiles and garlic; stir-fry until fragrant, about 10 seconds. Add beef and stir-fry until barely pink, about 2 minutes. Return green beans to wok and add sauce; cook, stirring, until sauce boils and thickens.

Makes 4 servings

A CUT ABOVE

I've always loved to use flavorful flank steak in beef stir-fries. Cut across the grain in thin slices and quickly cooked, it can be deliciously tender. It used to be one of the most economical cuts, but nowadays, as American cooks are exploring ethnic dishes like stir-fry and fajitas, the demand for flank steak has increased, and so has the price. Some other beef cuts that work well for stir-fry include: top sirloin, strip loin, ribeye, tri-tip and tenderloin.

185

A lighter, home-style version of the Sichuanese restaurant favorite, in which the beef is usually deep-fried and glazed with a thick sauce. I've turned it into a stir-fry with a light, sweet sauce that's every bit as tasty as the original.

TANGERINE PEEL BEEF

HOMEMADE APPEAL

The dried peel of tangerines and oranges is a flavoring staple in many Chinese dishes, particularly in the West, for a variety of meat and poultry dishes. You can buy it in bags at Chinese markets, but it's easy to make your own at home. After peeling the fruit, cut the peel into pieces, lay them out flat and cut or scrape away as much of the white pith from the inside of the peel as possible. Let the pieces of peel sun- or air-dry for a few days until they're firm but still flexible, then store them in an airtight jar.

2 pieces (each about 1 ½-inches square) dried tangerine peel

Marinade
2 tablespoons soy sauce
1 tablespoon cornstarch

¾ **pound flank steak, thinly sliced**

Sauce
⅓ cup orange juice
2 tablespoons rice wine
    or dry sherry
1 tablespoon soy sauce
½ teaspoon chili garlic sauce
2 teaspoons sugar
1 ½ teaspoons cornstarch

2 ½ tablespoons cooking oil
6 small dried red chiles
1 small onion, cut into 1-inch pieces
Orange slices for garnish

Method
1. Soak tangerine peel in warm water to cover until softened, about 15 minutes; drain. Thinly slice tangerine peel. Combine marinade ingredients in a bowl.

2. Add beef and stir to coat. Let stand for 10 minutes. Combine sauce ingredients in a bowl; set aside.

3. Place a wok over high heat until hot. Add 2 tablespoons oil, swirling to coat sides. Add chiles and cook, stirring, until fragrant, about 10 seconds. Add beef and stir-fry until barely pink, about 2 minutes. Remove the beef and chiles from the wok.

4. Add remaining ½ tablespoon oil to wok, swirling to coat sides. Add tangerine peel and onion; stir-fry for 1 minute. Add sauce and cook, stirring, until sauce boils and thickens.

5. Return beef and chiles to wok and cook until heated through. Remove to a serving plate and garnish with orange slices.

Makes 4 servings

A hearty, home-style stew—beef short ribs, slowly braised with root vegetables in a curried broth. I like to cook and serve this dish in a clay pot, but any large pot, such as a Dutch oven, can be used.

BRAISED SHORT RIBS IN A CLAY POT

SHORT STORY

Beef short ribs are one of my favorite cuts, and one that I find many people have never tried. They're rectangles of meat that contain a small, 1 to 2-inch piece of the rib bone. The bone and layers of fat in short ribs make them extremely flavorful. But they're also quite tough, so they must be cooked slowly with moist heat. Ask your butcher to cut them into pieces measuring about 1 inch by 2 inches to give dishes like this one a tra-ditional Chinese appearance.

Marinade
2 tablespoons dark soy sauce
2 teaspoons cornstarch

1½ to 1¾ pounds beef short ribs
2 green onions
1 pound taro root or thin-skinned
    potatoes
2 medium carrots
    or 2 cups cubed daikon
2 tablespoons cooking oil
4 slices ginger, lightly crushed
3 cups chicken broth
¼ cup rice wine or dry sherry
3 tablespoons prepared curry sauce
1 whole star anise

Method
1. Combine marinade ingredients in a bowl. Add short ribs and stir to coat. Let stand for 10 minutes. Cut green onions into 2-inch pieces. Peel taro and cut into 1-inch pieces. Roll cut carrots.

2. Place a wok over high heat until hot. Add oil, swirling to coat sides. Add ginger and green onions; cook, stirring, until fragrant, about 10 sec-onds. Add short ribs and cook until browned on all sides, 3 to 4 minutes.

3. Remove short ribs, ginger, and green onions from pan drippings and place in a a clay pot or a large pot. Add broth, wine, curry sauce, and star anise; bring to a boil over medium heat.

4. Reduce heat to low, cover, and simmer until meat is tender, about 1½ hours. Add taro and carrots, cover, and simmer until vegetables are tender, about 20 minutes.

Makes 4 to 6 servings

Venison stir-fried with leeks or onions is the kind of dish you might find in the province of Yunnan, to the south and west of Sichuan. Separated from central and coastal China by tall mountains, this remote region has developed its own unique cuisine. The most famous local specialty is Yunnan ham, but many dishes also feature a variety of exotic ingredients, like snails, sparrows and bear's paws, along with the meat of game animals, such as venison, rabbit and armadillo.

VENISON WITH LEEKS

¾ pound venison steaks,
about ½-inch thick

Marinade
2 tablespoons oyster flavored sauce
2 teaspoons cornstarch

Sauce
2 tablespoons hoisin sauce
1 tablespoon rice wine or dry sherry
1 teaspoon dark soy sauce
1 teaspoon chili garlic sauce

1 leek (white part only), julienned
2 tablespoons cooking oil
2 teaspoons minced garlic

Method

1. Thinly slice venison. Combine marinade ingredients in a bowl. Add venison and stir to coat. Let stand for 10 minutes. Combine sauce ingredients in a bowl; set aside.

2. Parboil leek in a pot of boiling water for 1 minute; drain.

3. Place a wok over high heat until hot. Add oil, swirling to coat sides. Add garlic and cook, stirring, until fragrant, about 10 seconds. Add venison and stir-fry until no longer pink, 1½ to 2 minutes. Add leek and sauce; cook until heated through.

Makes 4 servings

LEEK TIPS

When buying leeks, look for bright green leaves and a clean, firm white portion. Grit and mud often get trapped between the layers of leeks, so it's important to clean them thoroughly before using them in cooking. Start by cutting off and discarding the dark green tops and the root end, then cut an "X" in the root end about two inches deep. Rinse the leeks thoroughly under cold water, spreading out the layers at the root end and forcing water between them until the leek is completely clean.

A simple Sichuan-style dish that makes a colorful first course or a light meal-in-a-bowl. Humble vegetables become treasures when you julienne them and serve them with egg noodles in a savory broth.

EIGHT PRECIOUS NOODLE SOUP

EGG SHREDS

Chinese cooks often use lacy ribbons of cooked egg as a garnish. To make them, beat 2 eggs with a pinch of salt. Heat an 8-inch, non-stick frying pan over medium heat. Add ¼ teaspoon cooking oil to pan. Pour in ⅓ of eggs and swirl pan to cover entire bottom. Cook until egg is lightly browned on bottom and set on top, about 1 minute. Turn sheet over and cook 5 seconds; slide out of pan. Repeat to make 2 more egg sheets. When sheets are cool, cut in half, stack and slice crosswise into ⅛-inch shreds.

1 package (about 12 ounces) fresh Chinese egg noodles
8 asparagus spears, thinly sliced diagonally
½ cup each julienned bamboo shoots and carrots
½ cup each julienned celery and green onions
½ cup egg shreds (see column at left)
¼ cup julienned Sichuan preserved vegetable
3½ cups chicken broth
2 tablespoons oyster flavored sauce
2 tablespoons soy sauce
1 teaspoon chili garlic sauce
Toasted sesame seeds for garnish

Method

1. Cook noodles in a pot of boiling water according to package directions. Drain, rinse with cold water, and drain again. Place noodles into 4 soup bowls or 1 large serving bowl.

2. Parboil asparagus, bamboo shoots, and carrots separately in a pot of boiling water for 2 minutes. Drain each, rinse with cold water, and drain again. Arrange asparagus, bamboo shoots, carrots, celery, green onions, egg shreds, and preserved vegetable decoratively over noodles.

3. Combine broth, oyster flavored sauce, soy sauce, and chili garlic sauce in a saucepan; bring to a boil. Pour sauce over noodles and garnish with toasted sesame seeds.

Makes 4 servings

This is perhaps the most famous of Sichuan's street foods, and there are many variations on the basic formula of egg noodles with a spicy, creamy sesame sauce. My version includes minced meat and a last-minute sprinkling of chopped Sichuan preserved vegetables.

DAN DAN NOODLES

Marinade
2 tablespoons rice wine
    or dry sherry
2 tablespoons soy sauce
2 teaspoons cornstarch

½ pound minced lean chicken,
    pork, or beef

Sauce
½ cup sesame seed paste
3 tablespoons chicken broth
2 tablespoons oyster flavored sauce
1 tablespoon soy sauce
1 tablespoon rice vinegar
2 teaspoons chili garlic sauce

1 package (about 12 ounces) fresh
    Chinese egg noodles
1 tablespoon cooking oil
    Chopped Sichuan preserved
Vegetable for garnish

Method
1. Combine marinade ingredients in a bowl. Add chicken and mix well. Let stand for 10 minutes. Combine sauce ingredients in a bowl and whisk until blended; set aside.

2. Cook noodles in a pot of boiling water according to package directions. Drain, rinse with cold water, and drain again. Place noodles in a serving bowl.

3. Place a wok over high heat until hot. Add oil, swirling to coat sides. Add chicken and stir-fry for 2 minutes. Add sauce and cook until heated through. Pour sauce over noodles and garnish with Sichuan preserved vegetable.

Makes 4 servings

DAN DAN DERIVATIONS
The origin of Dan Dan noodles has passed into legend. Some say it all began with a street vendor in Sichuan who carried his entire portable kitchen on his back, using a contraption called a *dan*. Others claim that the name Dan Dan imitates the sound of the noodle vendors who announce their arrival by walking up and down the street clapping their hands. As for me, I'm content to simply say that Dan Dan means delicious, and leave it at that!

Noodling around at a curbside restaurant.

*S*picy pressed bean curd adds texture and flavor to this sweet-hot stir-fry of meat and vegetables, served over egg noodles.

NOODLES WITH SPICY BEAN CURD SAUCE

½ pound boneless chicken,
    pork, or beef
1 tablespoon oyster-flavored sauce

Sauce
¼ cup chicken broth
3 tablespoons hoisin sauce
3 tablespoons ketchup
1 tablespoon soy sauce
1 tablespoon chili garlic sauce

1 package (about 12 ounces) fresh
    Chinese egg noodles
2 tablespoons cooking oil
4 ounces spicy pressed bean curd,
    cut into ½-inch cubes
1 cup ½-inch cubes bamboo shoots
½ carrot, cut into ½-inch cubes
¼ cup frozen peas, thawed

Method

1. Cut chicken into ½-inch pieces. Place in a bowl and add oyster-flavored sauce; stir to coat. Let stand for 10 minutes. Combine sauce ingredients in a bowl; set aside.

2. Cook noodles in a pot of boiling water according to package directions. Drain, rinse with cold water, and drain again. Place noodles in a serving bowl.

3. Place a wok over high heat until hot. Add oil, swirling to coat sides. Add chicken and stir-fry for 1½ minutes. Add pressed bean curd, bamboo shoots, carrot, and peas; cook until carrot is crisp-tender, 1½ to 2 minutes.

4. Add sauce and cook until heated through. Pour sauce over noodles.

Makes 4 servings

BEYOND BEAN CURD

So, you've mastered tofu. What's next on the bean curd horizon? Try some of these on for size: *pressed bean curd* is firm and chewy, and comes marinated in a variety of seasonings. *Fermented bean curd,* sold in jars, has a mild wine-like flavor. *Bean curd sheets* are the dried skin that forms on the surface of soy milk during bean curd production. They're used as wrappers for meat and vegetable fillings, and added to soups and stews. *Deep-fried bean curd puffs* are used to add a meat-like texture to dishes, and you can often find ready-made puffs in Asian markets.

OK, I admit it. I don't eat Chinese food every night. Sometimes I take a break and order a good old-fashioned pizza. But what if pizza were Chinese? Chances are, it would taste a lot like this.

CHINESE PIZZA

CHINESE SAUSAGE

In Chinese delis, you often see slim, reddish-brown sausage links called *lop cheong* hanging in the window. They're most often made from pork, though some contain duck liver or chicken, and they're sold in pairs, held together by a colored string (the color identifies the type of sausage you're buying) or in vacuum-packed plastic packages. Seasoned with salt, sugar and rice wine, these sausages have a sweet-savory flavor that makes a nice complement to rice and vegetable dishes. They must be cooked before eating.

Dough
¼ cup warm water (110°F)
1 package (¼ ounce) active dry yeast
¾ cup water
2 tablespoons cooking oil
1 tablespoon honey
3 cups all-purpose flour
1 teaspoon salt

Sauce
⅔ cup tomato sauce
2 tablespoons chili garlic sauce
1½ tablespoons char siu sauce
1½ tablespoons hoisin sauce

Toppings
2 Chinese sausages (each about 2 ounces), thinly sliced diagonally
½ cup shredded roast duck meat
1 red bell pepper, julienned
4 green onions, sliced
8 white button mushrooms, sliced
1½ cups shredded mozzarella cheese

Method
1. Pour warm water into a bowl. Sprinkle yeast over water and stir until dissolved. Let stand until bubbles form, about 10 minutes. Combine water, oil, and honey in a bowl or measuring cup; set aside. Combine sauce ingredients in a bowl; set aside.

2. Place flour and salt in a food processor fitted with a metal blade; process for 10 seconds. With food processor running, pour water mixture down feed tube. With motor still running, pour dissolved yeast down feed tube. Process until mixture forms a ball. Remove to a lightly floured board; knead dough until smooth and elastic, about 5 minutes.

3. Place dough in a lightly greased bowl; turn to coat. Cover bowl with a dry towel. Let rise in a warm area until dough has doubled in bulk, about 1 hour.

4. Punch dough down. Divide dough in half. Flatten each half and roll out to form a 12-inch circle. Transfer each circle to a greased 12-inch pizza pan; pat dough firmly into pan edge.

5. To assemble each pizza, spread half of sauce over dough. Arrange half of toppings, except cheese, over sauce. Sprinkle evenly with half of cheese.

6. Preheat oven to 450°F. Bake pizza, one at a time, in lower third of oven until cheese melts and bottom of crust is browned, about 15 minutes.

These delicate dumplings with a soft, chewy dough and a sweet coconut filling make a nice finale for a buffet or sit-down dinner, brought right to the table in the bamboo steamer basket in which they were cooked.

CRYSTAL COCONUT DUMPLINGS

1⅓ cups wheat starch
⅓ cup cornstarch
¼ teaspoon salt
1 cup boiling water
1 tablespoon cooking oil

Filling
⅔ cup flaked coconut
⅔ cup finely chopped walnuts
¼ cup sugar
2 tablespoons butter, softened

Method
1. Combine wheat starch, cornstarch, and salt in a bowl. Add boiling water and oil, stirring with chopsticks or a fork, until dough holds together. Add 1 to 2 tablespoons more boiling water if necessary. On a lightly floured board, knead dough until smooth and satiny, about 5 minutes. Cover and let rest for 30 minutes.

2. Combine filling ingredients in a small bowl.

3. On a lightly floured board, roll dough into a cylinder then cut into 30 portions. To make each dumpling, roll a portion of dough to make a 3-inch to 3½-inch circle, about ⅛-inch thick; keep remaining dough covered to prevent drying. Place a teaspoon of filling in center of dough. Gather edges of dough around filling; pinch and pleat to seal.

4. Place dumplings, one half at a time, seam side up, in a heat-proof glass pie dish. Let dumplings rest for at least 5 minutes before steaming. Prepare a wok for steaming (see page 29). Cover and steam over high heat, about 8 minutes.

Makes 30

PICKING COCONUTS

When shopping for coconuts, choose those that feel heavy and full of liquid. Make sure the three "eyes" at one end of the coconut look dry with no signs of mold. When you're ready to open the coconut, pierce the eyes with an ice pick or a hammer and a heavy nail. Drain the coconut water, then use a hammer to break the coconut open. Pry the meat from the shell with a small knife and, if desired, scrape off the brown inner skin. Chop the meat by hand or use a blender or food processor to grate it.

These are the flaky short-dough cookies you find in Chinese bakeries all over the world. My version replaces the traditional lard with a combination of butter and shortening, producing a crisper, more tender cookie.

WALNUT COOKIES

NUTS ABOUT WALNUTS

The people of Sichuan are crazy about nuts—especially walnuts. You'll find fried or toasted walnuts added to stir-fries and other dishes, chopped walnuts used as a coating for fried foods, and ground walnuts made into a variety of sweets. They're also eaten whole, sometimes glazed with honey or sugar, as a snack. They've been grown in China for more than 1,500 years, so I was surprised to find high quality walnuts at a market in Sichuan, imported all the way from the faraway and exotic United States!

1 ¾ cups all-purpose flour
¾ teaspoon baking powder
½ teaspoon baking soda
½ cup butter, softened
½ cup shortening
⅔ cup sugar
½ cup packed brown sugar
1 egg, lightly beaten
1 teaspoon vanilla extract
¼ cup finely chopped walnuts
About 40 walnut halves

Method
1. Sift flour, baking powder, and baking soda into a bowl.

2. Beat butter, shortening, sugar, and brown sugar in a bowl with an electric mixer until fluffy. Add egg and vanilla extract; beat until blended. Add flour mixture; mix well. Stir in walnuts.

Shape dough into a ball, cover with plastic wrap, and refrigerate for 1 hour or for up to 2 days.

3. Preheat oven to 350°F. Divide dough into fourths. Divide each fourth into 10 portions. Roll each portion into a ball then place 2 to 3 inches apart on an ungreased baking sheet. Press a walnut in center of each ball.

4. Bake for 14 to 16 minutes or until golden brown. Let cool on baking sheet for 5 minutes, then transfer to wire rack to cool completely. Store in an airtight container.

Makes 40

FRUITS AND VEGETABLES

Here's a quick look at some of the ingredients used in this book.

Asian pears are juicy like a pear, crisp like an apple, and are also known as apple pears. They have a squatty look of an apple, a sandy texture, and a speckled yellow green or light brown skin of a pear. Generally they are blander in flavor than European pears.

Bean sprouts, both mung and soy bean sprouts, have bright silver bodies with yellow heads and long tails. Soy bean sprouts have larger heads and are crunchier in comparison to mung bean sprouts. It is best to use these the same day they are purchased, but they will last for a couple of days if kept refrigerated in an open bag.

Bok choy is a loose-leafed cabbage with thick white stalks and dark green leaves. Stalks have a mildly tangy taste and a crunchy texture. Leaves are peppery and soft. Baby bok choy is a smaller, younger version of bok choy. Shanghai baby bok choy is another variety which is jade green with spoon-shaped stalks and curved leaves. Both baby varieties are sweeter and less fibrous than regular bok choy.

Chiles (fresh). Generally, the smaller the chili, the hotter it is. The tiny 1½-inch Thai bird chili is one of the hottest available. The slightly larger serrano is just a bit milder, followed by the broad shouldered jalapeño. Remember to wash your hands after handling; their oils may burn or irritate your skin.

Chinese broccoli is a thin, dusty green stemmed, deep green leaved vegetable with tiny white flowers. When cooked, the tender stems and leaves have a slight bitter-sweet taste. Buy those with thin stems as larger stems tend to be older, more fibrous, and bitter tasting.

Chinese & Japanese turnips look like over-sized carrots but are grey-green-white in color. The Japanese variety is called daikon or giant white radish. There are many varieties available, but all taste sweet and peppery. Choose small, short turnips as longer turnips tend to be older and more fibrous.

Cilantro, also known as fresh coriander or Chinese parsley, is aromatic and has a distinct, refreshing flavor. Don't confuse cilantro with Italian parsley. Cilantro is the one with wide, flat leaves. Choose bright, perky bunches with fresh crisp leaves and stems. To store, stand cilantro in a glass of water and loosely cover the tops with a plastic bag and refrigerate.

Ginger looks like a knobby hand with shiny, smooth, golden skin and a fibrous, yellow-green interior. It has a spicy bite and a tantalizing aroma. Seasonal young ginger has a smoother, more delicate flavor and a less fibrous texture. Choose ginger that is hard, heavy, and free of wrinkles and mold.

Jícama looks like the world's largest turnip, with a tan, leathery skin and a crunchy, slightly sweet, white flesh. Although a bit more fibrous and not as sweet tasting, it is a good substitute for fresh water chestnuts. Choose small, firm, well-rounded jícama that are free of blemishes and mold.

Lemongrass looks like a long, woody green onion that is pale yellow-green in color. When cooked, it imparts a delicate lemony flavor and aroma. Use only the bottom 6 inches for cooking. Discard the top and remove the fibrous layer if it looks dry.

Lotus root looks like a long, thick, off-white, hard sausage. Just peel and slice crosswise to reveal an interesting cross-section showing the air holes that run the length of the root. Lotus root adds a fibrous crunch to soups and braised dishes.

Mushrooms (fresh) are available in several different types and are popular in Chinese cooking. The delicate, shell-shaped oyster mushroom, the long-stemmed, tiny-capped *enoki* mushroom, and the firm, golden brown *shiitake* mushroom. Oyster mushrooms and enoki mushrooms have a mild, delicate flavor; shiitake mushrooms have a rich, meaty flavor. All are smooth and velvety in texture.

Napa cabbage is commonly available in two types: the short, foot-ball-shaped Chinese napa cabbage, and the tall, bouquet-shaped Japanese napa cabbage. Both have sweet creamy white stalks with frayed, ruffled, pale green edges. Choose cabbages with moist, pale green leaves with no brown edges. Ignore the black spots found on the base as they are the result of unpredictable growing conditions.

Snow peas are flat pea pods with a sweet, sugary flavor and crisp, crunchy texture. Although they are completely edible and do not need to be shelled, it is best to snap off the stem ends and remove the fibrous strings that run along the sides. Choose young snow peas that are bright green, flat, crisp, and free of blemishes.

Sugar snap peas, like snow peas, are completely edible and do not need to be shelled. It is also best when the stem ends and the fibrous strings are removed. Thick, crunchy pods are sugary sweet when cooked. Buy young peas that are small as older, larger peas tend to be tough and fibrous.

Taro root is available in two types, including the large melon-sized taro and the small golf ball-sized taro. All are somewhat hairy, dark-skinned, and rough textured on the outside. The flesh ranges in color from white or grayish to light purple when cooked. Starchy in texture, cooked taro root is sweet and nutty in flavor. Choose those that are free of dents, wrinkles, blemishes, and mold.

RICE, NOODLES, FLOURS AND STARCH

Fresh products are available in the refrigerated section of most markets. Check individual packages for storage information. When working with wrappers, take out only a few at a time and cover the rest with a damp cloth to prevent them from drying. Dried products can be found on the shelf. Store dried products in a tightly sealed container in a cool, dry place. Most will keep for several months.

Bean thread noodles (dried) are a semi-transparent noodle made from mung bean starch that is available in a number of different lengths and thicknesses. Before using in soups and braised dishes, soak noodles in warm water until softened. Before deep-frying, separate a bundle of noodles inside a paper bag. Deep-fry small handfuls at a time.

Chinese egg noodles (fresh) are used throughout China, but are most popular in the Northern region where wheat grows more abundantly than rice. Available in dozens of varying widths, sizes and flavors in the refrigerator section. Cook according to individual package directions.

Egg roll wrappers are thin, pliable sheets of dough made from wheat flour, eggs, and water. When deep-fried, egg roll wrappers have a bubbly surface and are semi-crisp in texture.

Glutinous rice flour or sweet rice flour is made from ground glutinous rice. It is used most often to make dim sum doughs. When boiled, glutinous rice flour doughs become smooth and chewy in texture. Deep-frying the dough which usually encases a sweet paste or savory meat filling, yields a crisp, golden brown outside and a sweet and sticky inside.

Gyoza wrappers are pasta circles made from wheat flour, water, and eggs. The round wrappers can be used to wrap fillings for gyoza, potstickers, and siu mai and can be deep-fried, pan-fried, or steamed.

RICE

Glutinous rice, a variety of short-grain rice, resembles an opaque white, rice-shaped pearl. When cooked it becomes soft, moist, sweet, sticky, and translucent.

Long-grain rice is one of the most basic foods used throughout China. Long-grain rice is the least starchy of all rice varieties and cooks up dry and fluffy with grains that separate easily. These characteristics make it the ideal rice for fried rice recipes.

Medium-grain rice is shorter in length compared to long-grain rice and is a popular favorite in eastern areas of China. When cooked, medium-grain rice is shinier, stickier, and nuttier in texture.

Rice crusts are thin, hard, 1½-inch wafers of dried cooked long-grain or medium-grain rice which are deep-fried to yield a puffy, light, slightly crunchy square that is three times its original size. Rice crusts have a taste and texture similar to American rice cake snacks.

Rice flour is made from ground long-grain rice, and is most often used in doughs that make rice paper, rice noodles, and steamed cakes.

Rice noodles (fresh) are made from long-grain rice flour and are soft, pliable, and milky white. Available in whole folded sheets, wide cut strips, or as thin spaghetti-like strands coated with a light layer of oil to prevent them from sticking. Before using, rinse them gently in boiling water to soften the noodles and to remove the oily coating.

Rice noodles (dried) are made from long-grain rice flour and are stiff, brittle, and available in varying widths and lengths. Before using, soak dried rice noodles warm water until softened. Use soaked noodles in soups, salads, and clay pot dishes. Deep-fry rice sticks and use as a garnish around stir-fries or tossed into salads.

Rice paper is a brittle, semi-transparent round or a triangular sheet made from rice flour. Before using, soften rice papers between folds of a dampened towel until softened. Wrap meats and vegetables and eat out of hand or deep-fry until golden brown.

Spring roll wrappers are paper-thin pancakes made from a thin batter of wheat flour. When deep-fried, spring roll wrappers become crisp and smooth with a light-texture.

Tapioca starch (or pearls) is a fine, waxy-textured white powder made from the root of the cassava plant. Tapioca starch is used as a thickener and in combination with other flours to make dim sum doughs. Tapioca pearls of various sizes are used to make creamy puddings and sweet desserts.

Wheat starch is wheat flour with all the gluten removed. It is fine textured, off-white in color, and commonly used to make dim sum doughs. When steamed, wheat starch doughs become soft, shiny, and opaque white.

Wonton wrappers are pasta squares made from wheat flour, water, and eggs. Thick wrappers are used for deep-frying, pan-frying, or steaming. Thin wrappers are used in soups.

SAUCES AND PASTES

Sauces with a greater proportion of whole ingredients are generally thicker and referred to as pastes. Sauces and pastes of the same name are used interchangeably depending on the desired appearance of the final product. Both are found in various sized bottles and jars. Once opened, they should be refrigerated. Most will keep for several months to a year.

Barbecue sauce or char siu sauce is a thick jam-like sauce made from fermented soy beans, vinegar, tomato paste, chili, garlic, sugar, and other spices. It adds a sweet and spicy taste to grilled and roasted meats and poultry.

Black bean sauce is a ready-to-use sauce made from salted black beans and rice wine. Depending on the variety, black bean sauce may contain garlic or hot chiles. Just add the prepared sauce to stir-fries and sauces and heat through.

Black vinegar is made from the fermentation of a mixture of rice, wheat, millet or sorghum. Compared to common white vinegar, black vinegar is less tart, smokier, sweeter, more flavorful, and of course darker in color. A popular black vinegar from Eastern China is called *Chinkiang* vinegar.

Brown bean sauce is a thick, salty brown sauce made from whole and/or ground fermented soy beans. Brown bean sauce with the addition of hot chiles is called hot bean sauce and is mildly spicy.

Chili oil is a hot, reddish orange oil made by infusing the heat and flavor of whole dried chiles and red pepper flakes into oil. It is used as a flavoring agent and as a table condiment for those who like to add a spicy bite to any food.

Chili sauce is made from a blend of fresh and dried chiles and vinegar. Depending on the country of origin, different seasonings are added to give each a unique flavor. Some additional ingredients include garlic, ginger, soy beans, and sesame oil, to name only a few.

Curry generally defines a highly seasoned mixture of various ingredients. There are many prepared sauces and powders on the market. Generally, red curry contains a greater portion of dried red chiles, green curry contains more fresh green chiles, and yellow curry contains a blend of various dried spices.

Fermented bean curd is a soft and creamy curd with a smooth, thick custard-like texture, and a mildly pungent, wine-like aroma. White fermented bean curd contains sesame oil, rice wine, or chile and is used as a table condiment or to season vegetables. Red fermented bean curd,

flavored with red rice, rice wine, chili, or rose essence, is used to flavor meat and poultry dishes.

Hoisin sauce is a thick, granular sauce made from fermented soy beans, vinegar, garlic, sugar, and spices. It lends a spicy-sweet flavor and a deep, rich reddish brown color to roasts, stir-fries, and barbecues.

Oyster-flavored sauce is a thick, dark brown all-purpose seasoning sauce made from oyster extracts, sugar, and seasonings. Its distinct sweet-smoky flavor goes well in any meat and vegetable stir-fry. Hot and vegetarian variations are available.

Plum sauce is a light, amber sauce made from salted plums, apricots, yams, rice vinegar, chiles, and other spices. The sweet-tart, chunky jam-like sauce is often served with roast duck, barbecued meats, and deep-fried appetizers.

Rice vinegar is a mild, sweet vinegar made from rice. Popular Chinese and Japanese vinegars range in color from clear or slightly golden to rich amber brown. Seasoned rice vinegar is rice vinegar that has been sweetened with sugar.

Rice wine is a rich amber-colored liquid made from fermented glutinous rice and millet. It is aged 10 to 100 years to achieve its rich full-bodied flavor. Shao Hsing, a city in Eastern China, produces some of the best quality wines which are often specifically called for in Chinese cookbooks.

Sesame oil is a dark amber oil pressed from toasted white sesame seeds. Sesame oil is used in small amounts solely as a flavoring agent. The best sesame oils are labeled as 100 percent pure. Sesame oil adds a nutty taste and aroma to marinades, dressings, and stir-fries.

Sesame seed paste is a thick, cement-like paste made from toasted white sesame seeds. Used in Sichuanese cooking, it adds a nutty taste and aroma to foods. To use, discard the oil layer and remove the needed portion of paste. Replace the protective oil layer with fresh oil toprevent the paste from drying out. When making dressings, sauces, or marinades it is best to mix the paste with a little oil or water before adding the remaining ingredients.

Shrimp sauce is a pinkish gray sauce made from fermented shrimp. Don't let the pungent odor throw you off. Once it's cooked, the odor disappears leaving a salty, mellow, fish flavor. Shrimp sauce is often used as a seasoning in stir-fries and clay pot cooking.

SOY SAUCE

Dark soy sauce is regular soy sauce with the addition of molasses. Dark soy sauce is thicker, darker, sweeter, and more full-bodied in flavor. It is used when a richer flavor and deep mahogany color is desired.

Reduced-sodium soy sauce is the same as regular soy sauce but with a sodium reduction of approximately 40 percent. Also known as reduced sodium or lite soy sauce, it tastes less salty but still has all the rich flavor of regular soy sauce.

Regular soy sauce is the ingredient that gives Chinese dishes their characteristic flavor and rich brown color. Many types of soy sauce are available with different colors, aromas, and flavors, but all are made from soy beans and wheat using the same basic natural fermentation process.

Thin soy sauce is lighter in color, saltier in flavor, and thinner in consistency than regular soy sauce. It is used when little to no color change in the food is desired, such as when cooking poultry and vegetable dishes.

Sweet and sour sauce is a prepared sauce simply made from vinegar and sugar. Cantonese versions are fruitier. Other popular additions include chili, ketchup and ginger.

Sweet bean sauce is a thick, salty-sweet brown sauce made from fermented soy beans and sugar. Often used as a condiment for Peking Duck and Mu Shu dishes, but also used in marinades and stir-fries. It is not the same as sweet red bean paste which is commonly used as a pastry filling.

Sweet lotus seed paste is made from lotus seeds that have been cooked, mashed, and sweetened with sugar. It is most often used as a sweet filling in steamed and baked pastries and buns.

Sweet red bean paste shouldn't be confused with sweet bean sauce which is made from sugar-sweetened fermented soy beans. Sweet red bean paste is made from sweetened red beans and is used as a filling for both sweet and savory treats.

DRY SEASONINGS

Store dry seasonings in a tightly sealed container in a cool, dry place. Most will keep for several months.

Brown slab sugar is a caramel-colored slab made from compressed layers of semi-refined brown sugar, white sugar, and honey. Slabs typically measure 3 to 5 inches in length and are found in 1-pound portions wrapped in plastic packages. Place slabs in a plastic bag and crush with a rolling pin into a manageable measuring size.

Chinese five-spice is a cocoa-colored powder made from a combination of cinnamon, star anise, fennel, clove, ginger, licorice, Sichuan peppercorn, and dried tangerine peel. Found in small plastic packages and jars.

Chinese hot mustard is a pungent, fiery-flavored condiment often served with deep-fried appetizers. Dried powders are found in plastic packages. Prepared mustards are usually available in jars. Once opened, prepared mustard should be refrigerated.

Jujubes (dried) are a small, wrinkled red fruit resembling a large raisin with a sweet-tart apple taste. They are most often used in soups, braised dishes, or in a sweet pastry filling. Dried jujubes are also known as Chinese red dates.

Red chiles (small dried) are fiery hot. Use whole or break into smaller pieces. Crushed red pepper flakes are chopped whole dried red chiles. Remember to wash your hands after handling; their oils may burn or irritate your skin.

Rock sugar is a pale amber-colored crystals made from a combination of refined and unrefined sugars and honey. Found in plastic packages and cellophane-wrapped boxes. Place large pieces in a plastic bag and crush with a rolling pin into a manageable measuring size.

Salted black beans lend a distinctly pungent, smoky flavor to foods. To use, rinse whole beans under running water and lightly crush or coarsely chop. Salted black beans are available in plastic packages and should feel soft and not look dried out. Also known as preserved or fermented black beans.

Sichuan peppercorns are dried reddish brown berries that add a woodsy fragrance and leave a pleasantly numbing feeling in the mouth. To bring out their distinctive aroma and flavor, toast a few handfuls in a dry frying pan over low heat until fragrant. Use whole or crush in a spice grinder into a course or fine powder.

Star anise is an inedible, 1-inch star containing eight points, with each point encasing a shiny, mahogany-colored seed. If you can't find a whole pod, use eight broken points. Star anise adds a distinct spiced licorice flavor to rich braising sauces and stews.

Tangerine peel (dried) is a gnarled, brittle, rusty-orange-colored peel that adds a light citrus flavor to sauces, soups, and braised dishes. Before using, soak peels in warm water until softened. Scrape the underside with a table knife to remove the bitter white portion of the peel.

CANNED AND PRESERVED INGREDIENTS

Baby corn is mellow yellow-colored miniature ears of corn that are completely edible and have a sweet taste and a crunchy texture.

Bamboo shoots are available in several varieties including whole tips, young tips, sliced, or diced shoots. They all basically have a sweet taste but their texture varies due to the amount of fiber present in each cut. Young winter bamboo tips are most tender, and sliced shoots are most fibrous.

Black fungus (dried) is the all-encompassing name which includes cloud ear, wood ear, and a variety of other fungi. In their dried form, all look like old leather chips. Use only a few pieces of fungi at a time–their size will increase threefold with soaking. After soaking, the fungi have a crisp bite, a smooth, silky texture, and a bland taste.

Black mushrooms (dried) are also known as Chinese black mushrooms or Japanese dried *shiitake* mushrooms. All have brownish-black caps, tan undersides, a rich, meaty texture, and a wild mushroom flavor. Less expensive "winter" varieties are best for stir-fries and stuffing. For dishes that require whole mushrooms, "flower" mushrooms are best. These more expensive mushrooms have light tan creases in the cap and have a superior texture and richer flavor.

Ginger (preserved) is available in several types including crystallized and pickled ginger. Honey-colored, sugar-coated, crystallized ginger has a sweet-spicy flavor. Red pickled ginger is cured in a salt brine, then soaked in a sugar and vinegar solution.

Lychee (fresh) are available from July to September, and look like a bright, crimson pink berry with a bumpy, leathery peel. Remove the peel to reveal the semi-translucent, juicy flesh. Inside is a single, shiny, smooth, mahogany-colored seed. Both fresh and canned lychee are sugary sweet with a texture similar to soft grapes.

Sichuan preserved vegetable refers to a number of different spicy pickled Chinese vegetables including kohlrabi, mustard greens, napa cabbage, and turnips. Typically covered with a bit of chili powder and ground Sichuan peppercorns, they are dark olive-green in color with a spicy-salty taste. In traditional Chinese cooking, each vegetable is used in a different way, but for American tastes, all can be used interchangeably.

Straw mushrooms have a delicate sweetness and a firm, meaty texture. The unpeeled variety has a cap which encases the whole body and stem such that it resembles a little brown egg with a slightly flat bottom. The peeled variety has a brown, dome-shaped cap and a thick, straw-colored stem.

Water chestnuts (fresh) are squatty, 1½-inch, pointy-topped tubers with a shiny, inedible brown skin. Inside is the sweet, slightly starchy flesh. Canned water chestnuts have a similar texture but they are not as sweet. Buy fresh water chestnuts that are free of wrinkles and mold.

Before using canned vegetables, drain and rinse them under water to remove any trace of the salty canning liquid. If the vegetables have a metallic taste, blanch them in boiling water with a pinch of salt before cooking further.

OTHER TRADITIONAL INGREDIENTS

Want to learn more about ingredients? We've put together a handy guidebook called *Martin Yan's Simple Guide to Chinese Ingredients & Other Asian Specialties.* It takes the mystery out of shopping for common and exotic Asian ingredients. It's packed with color photos, cooking tips and storage information. And best of all, it's small enough to carry with you every time you shop. For more information, please contact: Yan Can Cook, P.O. Box 4755, Foster City, CA 94404. Fax: (415) 525-0522.

Agar agar is available in powder, rectangular, and strip forms. Feather-light rectangles are typically bright colored. Strips look like crumpled strands of cellophane tape. Powder and solid forms of agar agar need to be dissolved in hot water before being used as a jelling agent. Strips must be soaked in warm water before being added to salads.

Bamboo leaves are not actually eaten, but are used as a wrapper for savory stuffings. Most bamboo leaf dishes are grilled, steamed, or boiled leaving an aromatic, smoky flavor to the food. Sold dried in plastic packages, bamboo leaves should be soaked in warm water until softened.

Bean curd is available in three main types. All are made from soy beans and water, but each type varies slightly in texture. Soft bean curd is silky smooth and very light in texture. Firm and regular bean curds have more dense structures and slightly spongy interiors.

Chinese sausage, ranging from 4 to 6 inches in length, are deep red to brown in color and slightly bumpy in texture. Most are made from pork, pork fat, duck, or beef and are simply seasoned with salt, sugar, and rice wine. All are savory-sweet and must be cooked before eating.

Coconut milk can be used when good-quality fresh coconuts are not available. If a recipe calls for thick coconut milk or coconut cream, spoon off the thick layer from the top of an unshaken can. The liquid remaining in the bottom of the can is thin coconut milk. If a recipe just calls for coconut milk, shake the can and use the blended contents.

Panko are Japanese-style bread crumbs. These dried, toasted flakes are larger and coarser than Western-style bread crumbs. Panko is mainly used to coat deep-fried foods. After frying, panko is crunchy and does not have a greasy taste. Even after standing, panko retains its crisp texture.

Pressed bean curd is similar to fresh bean curd but more whey has been removed from the coagulated mixture of soy beans and water. Very firm and compact squares of pressed bean curd are available plain and marinated in different seasonings including soy sauce, star anise, Chinese five-spice, and sesame oil. Colors range from milky white to deep brown.

Seaweed, harvested from the sea, washed, dried, seasoned and packaged as deep green sheets is called *nori.* Before using, lightly toast the seaweed sheets until crisp and bright green then cut into the desired size. Nori sheets are usually used to wrap sushi or as a condiment sprinkled over hot cooked rice. Nori sheets are also available seasoned with hot spices and teriyaki flavors.

Sesame seeds, both black and white varieties, are used to flavor and garnish dishes. White sesame seeds, hulled and unhulled, have a sweet, nutty flavor. Black sesame seeds are slightly bitter. Unlike black sesame seeds, white sesame seeds should be toasted before using to intensify their flavor and aromatic fragrance.

YAN CAN COOK – LIST OF TELEVISION PROGRAMS

601. Food and Symbolism
Symbolism has always been important to the Chinese — a certain color, number, or shape can have far-reaching significance. Yan's trip to the Ming Tomb outside Beijing demonstrates the tomb's symbolism of peace and prosperity in the afterlife. Food in China is also symbolic. Martin reveals the symbolism expressed in *Minced Poultry with Walnuts in Lettuce Cups (p.72)*; *Braised Mushrooms with Scallops (p. 92)*; and *Porcupine Fish with Sweet Chili Sauce (p.100)*.

602. Homecoming
Yan brings his heart and wok back to his Chinese homeland, and samples some of his mother's home cooking. *Lotus Root with Seasonal Vegetables (p.134)*; *Ham and Vegetable Rice (p. 122)*; and *Honey-Lychee Chicken (p.112)* are just the right dishes to take Yan back to his roots, and he reminisces with a boat tour through the neighborhood of his grandmother's Eastern China farm land.

603. Wines of Shao Hsing
The people of Shao Hsing make their wine the traditional way, with a lot of pride and care, and Yan is there to see how it is done. He also goes to a wine bar to find "drunken food"— dishes that are cooked with wine. In the studio, Shao Hsing wine enhances the flavor of *Drunken Chicken (p.149)*; and *Drunken Crab with Ginger-Wine Sauce (p.141)*. It is even used in desserts, like a liqueur — witness Yan's *Poached Pears in Plum Wine (p.82)*.

604. Religion and Food
Many delightful vegetable dishes have their origin in the folklore of Buddhism, the pacifist nature of which advocates the preservation of life. When applied to the kitchen, this means a blossoming of vegetarian dishes, such as *Bean Curd with Sweet Tomato Sauce (p.98)*; *Nori Tofu Rolls (p.131)*; and *Peking Cabbage Pillows (p.61)*. Along the way, Yan takes viewers to religious sites in China, including the spectacular temples in Sichuan and the Longmen Grottos.

605. Food and Art
In China, where artists are revered, a learned scholar is educated in artistic disciplines, from poetry, to calligraphy, to the culinary arts. Yan gets creative with a feast of *Chicken Balls with Lychee Sauce (p.113)*; and *Shrimp Salad with Tropical Fruit Salsa (p.91)*. He also explores artistic expression at a cloisonné factory near Beijing, and at Splendid China, an Orlando, Florida theme park. Guest Clifford Chow of San Francisco's Harbor Village Restaurant gives tips on how to order in a Chinese restaurant.

606. Mongolian Cuisine
For centuries, the Chinese kept the Mongols north of the Great Wall, a 4,000-mile line of defense. When Genghis Khan's great Mongol army finally invaded in 1223 A.D., they brought with them a robust and hearty cuisine. Yan fires up the palate with a *Mongolian Hot Pot (p.76)*, suitable to the cold climate of Northern China; *Mongolian Roast Lamb (p.81)*; and wonderful baked buns that Yan calls *Sesame Seed Pillows (p.42)*.

607. Romantic Dinner
Many people express their love with poems and flowers. Yan does it the old fashioned way — with food! Nothing is more romantic than a quiet dinner for two, where Yan serves *Sizzling Oysters and Mussels (p.106)*; *The True Lover's Prawns (p.179)*; and a sweet conclusion, *Mango Pudding (p.124)*. Since a romantic dinner requires the right etiquette, Yan's friend June Ouellette helps him demonstrate. He also visits a tea ceremony in China, where tea can be a symbol of love, and offers a look at Chinese folk dancing.

608. Picnic on the West Lake
Beautiful, romantic West Lake is the perfect spot for a picnic. Yan visits the lake, long a source of artistic inspiration, and whips up the perfect foods for a picnic, including *Lotus Salmon Patty (p.139)* and *Braised Short Ribs*

608. Picnic on the West Lake (cont.)
in a Clay Pot (p.188). He also takes a look at the "Farmers' Painting" that is sweeping through China.

609. Day and Night of Shanghai
"The Paris of the East," Shanghai is the most modern and cosmopolitan of all Chinese cities. To get a feel for the city, Yan kicks up his heels with a few of its 16 million inhabitants and tries some of its food. *Wok-Smoked Fish (p.178)* with a touch of oolong tea flavor; *Lion's Head Meatballs (p.150)*; and *Open-Faced Omelet with Savory Garlic Sauce (p.58)* are a few local favorites.

610. Foods of Xian
Xian, the ancient capital of China, was one of the most influential cities of the past, culturally as important as ancient Rome. Today, it's a busy industrial city that blends the new with the old. Yan visits this very historic city and tours a local open air night market. He also prepares a local favorite, *Fragrant Peppercorn Tofu (p.169)*; as well as *Tangerine Peel Beef (p.186)*; and *Dan Dan Noodles (p.191)*.

611. The Cantonese Banquet
There is an old saying in China: "Eat in Canton." Canton, or Guangzhou, is the undisputed culinary capital of Southern China, and its cuisine has led the way for international appreciation of Chinese cooking. Yan's guest, Executive Chef Andy Wai of San Francisco's Harbor Village Restaurant, joins him as they prepare *Peking Roasted Duck (p.75)*; and *Pei Pa Duck (p.114)*. Yan also serves up *Steamed Fish with Sizzling Lemongrass Oil (p.177)*; and *Triple Pepper Steak (p.117)*, and takes us to a favorite Cantonese restaurant.

612. Buddhist Temple
The Shaolin Temple near Louyang has always been known in the West for its martial arts disciplines. But the temple is first and foremost the major pillar of Chinese Buddhism. Yan observes the temple's disciplined daily routine. But his favorite spot is the kitchen, where the monks prepare simple, nutritious vegetarian dishes that

Yan recreates: *Pea Pods with Pressed Bean Curd (p.94)*; *Braised Vegetable-Tofu Casserole (p.57)*; and *Tofu Custard with Tropical Fruits (p.127)*.

613. Cooking with Kids
In China, children are taught to help with household chores, and they learn early on how to help in the kitchen. Yan is assisted by some young friends in preparing special dishes that children will love to make with their parents: *Sichuan Pizza (p.194)*; *Chinese Barbecued Spareribs (p.120)*; and for dessert, *Lemony Tofu Custard (p.125)*. He also shows how children in China put their natural energy to good use with acrobatics and martial arts.

614. Streets of Beijing
Beijing is a vibrant city of 11 million people constantly on the move, and the culinary focal point of Guangzhou. Yan visits the famous Tianamen Square and the Beijing night market, where the streets are alive with the tantalizing aromas of all kinds of food. Yan recreates the dishes that can be found at curbside restaurants all over the city: *Hot and Sour Beijing Dumplings (p.48)*; *Green Onion Cakes (p.44)*; and *Chilled Vegetable Roll with Thin Pancake (p.56)*.

615. Chinese Health Food
Chinese cooking emphasizes the principles of Yin and Yang — contrasting elements in perfect balance. Yan cooks dishes that exemplify a balanced diet: *Double Steamed Chicken (p.183)*; *Chilled Tofu with Bean Sprouts (p.173)*; and *Asparagus with Sweet and Pungent Dressing (p.166)*. He also shows how the Chinese stay physically fit into their old age, by riding bicycles and doing Tai Chi.

616. Suzhou Banquet
In China, there is a saying, "In heaven there is paradise, on earth there is Suzhou." The ancient city is built on water, and with its canals, bridges, and many gardens, beautiful Suzhou has long charmed its visitors. Yan visits the famous Zhou Zhen Yuan garden, or "Garden of the Foolish Politician," and takes in the Suzhou Banquet. He

demonstrates such delectable dishes from the banquet as *Suzhou Pork in a Clay Pot (p.147)*; *Steamed Fish with Fiery Black Bean Sauce (p.101)*; and *Tri-Color Chicken and Vegetable Mold (p.148)*.

617. Foods of the Terracotta Warrior
Yan visits the burial chambers of the ancient emperor Qin Shi Huang, where archaeologists have unearthed more than 7,000 life-size terracotta figures, all with startling detail and in battle formation. His majesty did not leave behind a menu, so Yan designs a feast fit for a king and his army: *Hunan Beef with Dry-Fried Beans (p.185)*, spicy enough to wake up any sleeping taste buds; *Spicy Fun See Noodles (p.171)*; and Yan's own invention, *Glazed Xian Chicken (p.71)*.

618. Eight Precious Tea
In China, tea is more than the traditional beverage. The word "tea" describes health tonics and nutritious broths as well, such as Yan's *Fragrant Beef Soup (p.163)*, made with tea. Tea is used in all manner of cooking, as in *Mushroom Tea Rice (p.151)*, made with jasmine or green tea leaves; and *Tea-Smoked Chicken (p.181)*. Yan shows the etiquette of tea service and takes viewers to Sichuan to learn about the special Eight Precious Tea, then finishes with a relaxing *Sweet Date Tea (p.155)*.

619. Bamboo Story
In China, the versatile bamboo has a thousand uses, and nothing from the plant gets wasted. Bamboo shoots are used in Yan's *Braised Bamboo Shoots and Mushrooms (p.174)*; bamboo leaves are used as a wrapper for food, such as Yan's *Fish in Bamboo Leaf (p.105)*; and for special guest Chef Quen Wu of the Souzhou Pearl Restaurant in Orlando, Florida, the bamboo steamer is the perfect cooking utensil for making steamed *Scallop-Tofu Butterflies (p.67)*.

620. Duck Soup
Yan pays tribute to the duck — the Peking duck, that is, which embodies the elegance and grace of Northern Chinese cuisine. After exploring a duck farm in China's countryside, Yan makes his own *Roasted Homestyle Peking Duck (p.75)*; and its American cousin, *Lychee and Pineapple Duck (p.108)*. Then, Yan takes us to the Hui Zhen Restaurant near Beijing for their classic version of Peking Duck; and returns to the studio to make a delicious *Duck Soup (p.55)* from the leftovers.

621. Temple of Heaven
As a Chinese ritual, offerings of food are made to heavenly deities and ancient ancestors. Before the end of the lunar calendar, offerings are made to the Kitchen God. If the gods are generous, you are granted a prosperous new year. Yan offers viewers his steamed *Sweet Date Buns (p.154)*; *White-Cut Chicken with Pepper Salt (p.109)*; and *Vegetarian Delight (p.99)*. Along the way, he explains Confucianism and visits Beijing's Temple of Heaven, where ancient emperors made offerings.

622. Entertain at Home
Entertaining friends and family is a simple pleasure that we all enjoy. A good party needs planning, but not necessarily a lot of preparation, as Yan's good friend Chef Larry Chu explains. While Chef Chu sets up a beautiful buffet, Yan makes some party favorites: *Miniature Spring Rolls (p.49)*; *Ginger-Date Wontons (p.153)*; and *Eight-Piece Beijing Chicken (p.70)*. Yan also visits a Beijing Tea House, where local pleasure-seekers entertain guests away from home.

623. Wonders of the World
For thousands of years, China isolated itself from the world. Today, China has opened up its borders to look outward for new ideas, and is incorporating many Western influences. Foreign products have changed the way Chinese cook, as seen in such dishes as *Fish with Spicy Salsa (p.65)*; *Honey-Glazed Lemon Chicken (p.110)*; and *Honey Walnut Prawns (p.145)*. Yan also visits China's "Windows of the World" tourist attraction for an exploration of the two-way street of cultural exchange.

624. Dumpling Banquet
Dumplings, in some form or another, are popular all over the world. In China, there is even a banquet that was designed to serve nothing but dumplings. Yan demonstrates the many ways that dumplings can be prepared with his *Flower Petal Dumplings (p.51)*; and *Hot and Sour Dumplings in Chili Broth (p.158)*. He also enjoys the dumpling banquet, and shows how to order the small Chinese dishes known as Dim Sum.

625. A Day at the Farm
Outside of the large cities, millions of Chinese still dwell in small rural towns and villages, living their lives as they did centuries ago. Yan takes viewers to a farm near Louyang to see how the average Chinese family lives day to day. Along the way, he samples simple, hearty dishes like those enjoyed in the heartland, such as the classic Sichuan dish *Kung Pao Chicken (p.185)*, made with walnuts instead of peanuts; *Noodles with Spicy Bean Curd Sauce (p.193)*; and *Hot and Sour Soup with Lemongrass (p.159)*.

626. Shanghai Banquet
Shanghai is the embodiment of the old and the new, the east and the west of China. It aims to become the most cosmopolitan city on the continent by the next century. Yan takes us on a tour of the city and to the complex and sophisticated Shanghai Banquet, which can include such dishes as *Fish Tail in Brown Sauce (p.138)*; *Watercress Soup with Crab (p.89)*; and *Steamed Shanghai Buns (p.133)*.

627. Fast Food of Beijing
One of the best ways to see China is on foot. The streets of Beijing are full of life, noise, people, and food. At any time of day, enterprising sidewalk vendors put out fast, delicious dishes, which Yan shows how to prepare at home: *Beijing Wings (p.47)*; *Hot and Sour Beijing Dumplings (p.48)*; and *Beijing Noodle Soup (p.53)*. In Beijing, Yan finds a popular street food —"The Big Bowl of Tea."

628. Arts and Crafts
In China, many chefs are considered artisans. Art and food meet as Yan's guest, Chef James Leung, joins him to demonstrate beautiful garnishes and vegetable carvings for dishes that please the eye as well as the palate: *Silk Thread Chicken Salad (p.164)*; *Tofu Mosaic (p.135)*, prepared with fancy-cut tofu; and a beautiful *Mixed Vegetable Stir-Fry (p.136)*. Yan also takes a look at silk production and Shanghai's "Antique Street."

629. Ancient Xian Banquet
Xian was established 2,200 years ago by emperor Qui Shi Huang as the capital of China, a land he unified out of many warring states. In his burial vault were discovered amazing ancient artifacts. Yan visits replicas of the discoveries on display at Splendid China in Orlando, Florida. The famous Xian Banquet celebrates the ancient heritage of Xian. Yan celebrates the Xian Banquet with his *Sichuan-Style Cold Mixed Noodles (p.165)*; *Golden Meat-Filled Coins (p.52)*; and *Wok-Seared Lamb with Four Onions (p.80)*.

630. Multi-Ethnic Cuisine
We often think of China as one people and culture, but China actually has 54 ethnic minorities, each contributing to the country's culture, arts and language. This diversity is felt in the cuisine. Yan prepares *Mongolian Lamb Skewers (p.79)*; *Venison with Leeks (p.189)*, reflecting influence of the Manchu people; and *Curried Shrimp and Scallops (p.180)*, inspired by the Guanxi province. Yan also takes in a traditional Mask Changing dance at the Splendid China Parade.

631. Imperial Banquet
In imperial China, the 108-course royal banquet was hailed as the finest of all banquets. Yan reveals a few of its secrets: *Sweet and Sour Fish Rolls (p.96)*; *Braised Mushrooms and Tofu (p.174)*; and *Pei Pa Shrimp (p.86)*, so named because it resembles the melon lute called a pei pa. Special guest Min Xiao-Fen provides musical accompaniment on her pei pa. Yan also visits Beijing's Forbidden City — the royal palace — and the

Fang Shan Restaurant's elaborate multi-coursed Imperial Banquet.

632. Foods of Ancient Xian

The ancient city of Xian is recognized as the cradle of Chinese civilization. Yan explores the rich history and culinary heritage of the city, sampling the best local dishes, such as *Three Ginger Beef (p.115)*; and *Sizzling Rice Soup (p.161)*. After exploring the local Ban Po village just outside the city, Yan uses walnuts, which originated in China, to prepare *Braised Bean Curd with Walnuts (p.168)*.

633. Tea and Fortune

Tea is not only a perfect companion to Chinese dishes, but it is also a flavorful ingredient. Yan visits the most famous tea plantation in China, the Dragon Well plantation, near Hangzhou in Eastern China, then returns to the studio to cook up *Dragon Well Shrimp (p.144)*. Then Yan shares a pot of tea with his aunt in Shanghai, and introduces wonderful snacks that go well with tea: *Honey-Glazed Nut Snacks (p.83)*; and *Walnut Cookies (p.196)*.

634. Sichuan Banquet

In the West of China, there is a saying, "When you are hot, you must be in Sichuan!" In the hot, humid climate, local people perk up their foods with hot spices, primarily red chili pepper. And in Sichuan, chili pepper can be a religion. Yan samples a special Sichuan banquet featuring a *Warm Chicken Salad (p.172)*; *Seafood over Singing Rice (p.175)*, a medley of shrimp and scallops with a popping rice crust; and *Chicken and Egg White Scramble (p.74)*.

635. Waterways of Shao Hsing

Eastern China's ancient city of Shao Hsing has a picturesque grand canal system, earning the town its nickname "The Venice of the East," and it has always been a good place to enjoy food, song and the famous local rice wine. Yan visits a Shao Hsing winery, and enjoys fine cuisine — *West Lake Soup (p.130)*, a savory soup flavored with the local wine; *Fish Fillet in Wine Sauce (p.63)*; and *Shao Hsing Savory Prawns (p.145)*.

636. Southern Chinese Cooking

Southern China has been the center of recent Chinese economic expansion. As a trade center, Guangzhou has opened up to the West and has consequently adopted Western influences. In culinary terms, that means fusion, or East-meets-West, cuisine, such as *Prawn- Stuffed Lychees (p.105)*. Yan's *Two Broccoli Beef (p.118)* uses both Chinese and Western broccoli. *Steamed Spareribs in Plum Sauce (p.119)* is a more typical local favorite.

637. The Moving Feast

A Chinese banquet can be a moving experience — especially in Hangzhou, where they stage banquets on a boat. The Xi Hu, or West Lake, in Hangzhou is the most famous lake in China, and it has inspired famous writers and poets for centuries. Great beauty also inspires great cuisine, such as *Seafood in a Orange Basket (p.69)*; *Clear- Simmered West Lake Fish (p.140)*; and the subtle and delicate *Four-Color Vegetable Fan (p.62)*.

638. The People of Beijing

As the most populous country in the world, China is destined to have an exciting capital city. Yan tours historical Beijing, from Tianamen Square to the Forbidden City Market, one of the world's first farmer's markets. At the market, one can purchase the ingredients for these Beijing favorites: *Mongolian Beef (p.77)*; *Chicken and Walnut Croquettes (p.46)*; and *Steamed Garden Vegetables (p.95)*.

639. Water Banquet

In Louyang, Empress Wu Zetin of the Tang Dynasty, the only female sovereign in Chinese history, invented the 24-course Water Banquet, which has become a local tradition. Here, water means broth, as in *Mushrooms in Fragrant Broth (p.90)*; *Seafood Medley in Chili Broth (p.162)*; and *Eight Precious Noodle Soup (p.190)*. Yan visits the authentic Water Banquet at the Zen Pu Tom restaurant in Louyang and the ancient Grand Canal, built to expand the silk trade during the Tang Dynasty.

INDEX

PRODUCERS ACKNOWLEDGMENT

Making a television cooking series, such as the YAN CAN COOK show, depends on the harmonious collaboration of many people and dozens of talented individuals contribute to the process.

For their generosity and kind support, special thanks go to our funders and to those individuals and companies who donated their time, talent, food, furnishings and equipment in support of the sixth season of the YAN CAN COOK show. To the entire production team, those dedicated men and women whose expertise and professionalism are evident in each program you watch, I extend my heartfelt thanks.

Thanks to the following organizations and their dedicated staffs who shared their knowledge and resources:

MAPLE LEAF FARMS
MONTEREY MUSHROOMS
CALIFORNIA ASPARAGUS
    COMMISSION
CALIFORNIA CANTALOUPE
    ADVISORY BOARD
BARD VALLEY MEDJOOL DATE
    GROWERS ASSOCIATION
U.S. RICE COUNCIL

Food Provided by:
Chef Chu's Restaurant
Greenleaf Produce
Harbor Village Restaurant
Raley's/Bel Air
Royal Hawaiian Seafood
Royal Pacific Foods
Tesio Meat & Poultry
Wu Kong Restaurant

Special Thanks to:
Ah Sam Florists
Angray-Fantastico Corp.
Bernardaud
BiRite Food Service Distributors
Country Stark Java
General Electric Appliances
Folk Art Gallery–Larkspur
Flying Elephants–San Rafael
Man-U Imports
Oscartielle Equipment Co.
Pier One Imports
Pottery Barn
Republic Uniforms
Rosenthal China & Crystal
Russell Range
Takahashi Imports
Taylor & Ng
Thomas by Rosenthal
Zonal
Wing Sing Chong

Linda Brandt, Producer
YAN CAN COOK–The Best of China

SUPPORT YOUR LOCAL
PUBLIC BROADCASTING STATION!

**Public Television.
You make it happen!**

Every community across America is reached by one of the 346 member stations of the Public Broadcasting Service. These stations bring information, entertainment, and insight for the whole family.

Think about the programs you enjoy and remember most:
Mystery…Masterpiece Theatre…Nova…Nature…Sesame Street… Ghostwriter…Reading Rainbow…Baseball…The Civil War…MacNeil/Lehrer News Hour…Great Performances…National Geographic…Washington Week in Review…and so many more.

On your local PBS station, you'll also find fascinating adult education courses, provocative documentaries, great cooking and do-it-yourself programs, and thoughtful local analysis.

Many public television series—like *Yan Can Cook: The Best of China*—are underwritten by generous corporate citizens like those recognized in this book. But more than half of all public television budgets come from individual member support.

For less than the cost of a night at the movies, less than a couple of months of a daily paper, less than a month of your cable TV bill, you can help make possible all the quality programming you enjoy.

Become a member of your public broadcasting station and do your part.

TREATS FOR THE PALATE AND THE EYE

Enjoy more great cookbooks from the fascinating chefs you watch on PBS.

$15.95

"Pépin's principles are straightforward: cooking can be healthy, fast, easy, and fun." —*Food Arts*

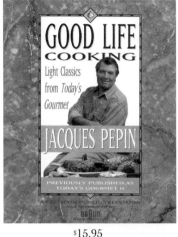

$15.95

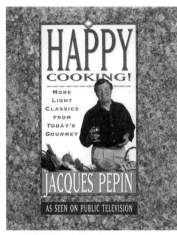

$16.95

"What Pépin does better than anyone else is make ordinary dishes delicious." —*Image Magazine*

From Hawaii's hottest young chef, a sensuous and intriguing introduction to the new cuisine of Hawaii.

$16.95

"Roy Yamaguchi is one of the first chefs to marry classical techniques with traditional Asian and Hawaiian ingredients....Now (this) companion volume makes it easy to learn how the different flavors of this cuisine complement one another" —*Bon Appétit*

Tempting recipes, and the professional techniques to make them come out just right, from the chefs of the California Culinary Academy.

$18.95

"*Cooking at the Academy* has been a delicious success." —*San Francisco Chronicle*

The China Travel Service

Conducting a culinary tour in Beijing.

CHINA TRAVEL SERVICE

香港 中国旅行社

How do you cover more than 65,000 miles in just three months? First, you need a great travel service! I'm particularly grateful to the China Travel Service of Hong Kong and the United States, for helping make my culinary journey a reality. From mapping out itineraries and travel plans to arranging for more than 100 meals and banquets, the outstanding CTS staff and management really went the extra mile for us. Their gracious, professional tour guides provided a wealth of information and took us off the beaten path to give us an insider's tour of China. If you ever have the good fortune to visit China, I hope you'll make the CTS a part of your travel plans.

In the middle of the Forbidden City at Splendid China.

Splendid China and Windows on the World

Thanks, also, to the management and staff of Splendid China, The Chinese Cultural Village and Windows on the World, the remarkable theme parks in Shenzen in southern China, and to their American cousin, the Splendid China theme park in Orlando, Florida, where you can see all of China in a single day—without ever leaving the U.S! Their support was invaluable to the production of many location segments for the *Yan Can Cook* show.

A Musical Note

In China, we have a saying: "Fine wine and food are nothing without fine music." The magnificent music used in the sixth season of *Yan Can Cook* on public television was composed by Noel Quinlan of The Sound Department, Hong Kong. The haunting melodies from his two CDs, *Middle Kingdom I & II* and *Natural World I, II & III*, provide a perfect audio backdrop for the sights, places and flavors of China.

Middle Kingdom II

For more information about The China Travel Service, Noel Quinlan's music, or Martin Yan's ingredient guide, please write to us: P.O. BOX 4755, FOSTER CITY, CA 94404, USA. (FAX: 415-525-0522).

A SPECIAL THANKS

You can't make a great meal without great ingredients. And the same goes for producing a cooking show or writing a cookbook. I'd like to express my deepest gratitude to four very special companies, whose generous support made possible the sixth season of the *Yan Can Cook* show on public television. They are truly the key ingredients of my recipe for success.

ABOUT MARTIN YAN

Celebrated Master Chinese Chef Martin Yan is a cooking teacher, a cookbook author, and host of the immensely popular television cooking series *Yan Can Cook*, recipient of the prestigious James Beard Award for "Best Television Cooking Show" in 1994.

Born in Guangzhou, China, Yan began his culinary career as a young Hong Kong restaurant apprentice and later graduated from the Overseas Institute of Cookery in Hong Kong. He went on to earn his M.S. in Food Science from the University of California at Davis. Moving to Canada, Yan received more extensive restaurant training and was certified as a Master Chinese Chef by the Ontario Chinese Restaurant Association.

Yan's first television appearance was on a Canadian talk show in 1978. He was such a hit, he was subsequently offered his own series, *The Yan Can Cook Show*—the beginning of a successful television career that has included more than 1,000 half hour cooking programs.

In 1982, public television station KQED began producing *Yan Can Cook* in San Francisco, and it has since become one of the most consistently popular cooking shows in America. The series reaches more than 85% of all households in the United States on public television and has been seen, or is currently seen, in more than 70 countries around the world.

As cooking instructor, Yan teaches Chinese and Asian cuisine at many top culinary institutions, including the California Culinary Academy, Johnson & Wales, the Culinary Institute of America, and the New England Culinary Academy. Since 1993, *Yan Can Cook* scholarship programs have been established in these schools.

In addition to hosting *Yan Can Cook* and teaching, Martin Yan is a restaurant and food consultant and a much sought-after public speaker. He frequently gives entertaining lectures and demonstrations at conventions, state fairs, professional trade shows, home and garden shows and charitable events.

Yan is the author of eight best-selling cookbooks.